THE HEART OF TAROT

An Intuitive Introspective Guide to Interpreting the Cards

Dr. Ruth A. Souther

Published by Crystal Heart Imprints
2945 Stanton, Springfield,
www.crystalheartimprints.com
Printed in the United States
All rights reserved
Copyright Dr. Ruth A. Souther
Revised Edition 2023
1st Printing 2012
ISBN: 978-09721003-1-1

*Dedicated to all those right souls with the courage
to journey into the archetypical
realm of inner knowledge.*

*May your path be heartfelt,
may your mind be uncluttered,
may your dreams be fulfilled,
may your life be enriched,
and may your travels be joyful!*

The Heart Of Tarot

TABLE OF CONTENTS

Page 5 – 6	How It All Began
Page 7 – 8	Tarot 101: Intro to the Mysteries
Page 9 – 11	What is an Archetype?

THE MAJOR ARCANA

Page 14	**The Quest – Discovering Self**
Page 16	Major Arcana Key Words
Page 17 – 18	0 – Fool
Page 19 – 20	1 – Magician
Page 21 – 22	2 – Priestess
Page 23 – 24	3 – Empress
Page 25 – 26	4 – Emperor
Page 27 – 28	5 – Hierophant
Page 29 – 30	6 – Lovers
Page 31 – 32	7 – Chariot
Page 33 – 34	8 – Adjustment
Page 35 – 36	9 – Hermit
Page 37 – 38	10 – Fortune
Page 39 – 40	11 – Lust
Page 41 – 42	12 – Hanged Man
Page 43 – 44	13 – Death
Page 45 – 46	14 – Art
Page 47 – 48	15 – Devil
Page 49 – 50	16 – Tower
Page 51 – 52	17 – Star
Page 53 – 54	18 – Moon
Page 55 – 56	19 – Sun
Page 57 – 58	20 – Aeon
Page 59 – 60	21 – Universe
Page 61 – 62	Protection

THE MINOR ARCANA

Page 64	**The Quest – Finding Balance**
Page 65	**Wands (Fire) – Authentic Self**
Page 66	Wands Key Words
Page 67 –	Ace of Wands
Page 69 – 70	Two of Wands
Page 71 – 72	Three of Wands
Page 73 – 74	Four of Wands
Page 75 – 76	Five of Wands
Page 77 – 78	Six of Wands
Page 79 – 80	Seven of Wands
Page 81 – 82	Eight of Wands
Page 83 – 84	Nine of Wands
Page 85 – 86	Ten of Wands

Page 87	**Swords (Air) – Mental Attitude**
Page 88	Swords Key Words
Page 89 – 90	Ace of Swords
Page 91 – 92	Two of Swords
Page 93 – 94	Three of Swords
Page 95 – 96	Four of Swords
Page 97 – 98	Five of Swords
Page 99 – 100	Six of Swords
Page 101 – 102	Seven of Swords
Page 103 – 104	Eight of Swords
Page 105 – 106	Nine of Swords
Page 107 – 108	Ten of Swords
Page 109	**Disks (Earth) – Physical Presence**
Page 110	Disks Key Words
Page 111 – 112	Ace of Disks
Page 113 – 114	Two of Disks
Page 115 – 116	Three of Disks
Page 117 – 118	Four of Disks
Page 119 – 120	Five of Disks
Page 121 – 122	Six of Disks
Page 123 – 124	Seven of Disks
Page 125 – 126	Eight of Disks
Page 127 – 128	Nine of Disks
Page 129 – 130	Ten of Disks
Page 131	**Cups (Water) – Emotional Identity**
Page 132	Cups Minor Arcana Key Words
Page 133 – 134	Ace of Cups
Page 135 – 136	Two of Cups
Page 137 – 138	Three of Cups
Page 139 – 140	Four of Cups
Page 141 – 142	Five of Cups
Page 143 – 144	Six of Cups
Page 145 – 146	Seven of Cups
Page 147 – 148	Eight of Cups
Page 149 – 150	Nine of Cups
Page 151 – 152	Ten of Cups
Page 153	**THE ROYALTY**
Page 154	**The Quest: Mastering Challenges**
Page 155	**What is the Royalty Challenge**
Page 156 - 158	**The Visionary Princess**
Page 159 – 162	Princess of Wands
Page 163 – 166	Princess of Swords
Page 167 – 170	Princess of Disks
Page 171 – 174	Princess of Cups

Page 175 -177	**The Designing Prince**
Page 178 – 181	Prince of Wands
Page 182 – 185	Prince of Swords
Page 186 – 189	Prince of Disks
Page 190 – 193	Prince of Cups
Page 194-196	**The Expanding Knight**
Page 197 – 199	Knight of Wands
Page 200 – 202	Knight of Swords
Page 203 – 206	Knight of Disks
Page 207 – 209	Knight of Cups
Page 210 - 212	**The Summoning Queen**
Page 213 – 215	Queen of Wands
Page 216 – 218	Queen of Swords
Page 219 – 221	Queen of Disks
Page 222 – 225	Queen of Cups

Numerology/Astrology References

Page 226 – 227	Numerology/Number Grid/Shadow Card
Page 228	Calculate Life Number
Page 229	Calculate Year Number
Page 230	Astrological Influences/Major Arcana
Page 231	Minor Arcana Astrological Influence

Card Spreads

Page 232	Astrological House Spread
Page 233	Positional Meanings for House Spread
Page 234	Astrological Signs Spread
Page 235	Positional Meanings for Signs Spread
Page 236	Elemental Spread/Positional Meanings
Page 237	Intuitive Tarot Card Spread
Page 238	Traditional Celtic Spread/Positional Meanings
Page 239	Year in Motion Spread/Positional Meanings

Bonus Section

Page 240 - 253	The Fool's Journey by Cynthea Jones
Page 254	Author Bio: Dr. Ruth A. Souther

Dr. Ruth A. Souther

HOW IT ALL BEGAN

The images and meanings of Tarot describe you on your life path and the endless, universal possibilities reflected in the night sky. It is the same path I've been on for the past twenty years while learning about Tarot - a course I'm still following. During that time, I struggled with the concepts of Tarot, mainly how it works.

I could not explain why a simple deck of cards with pictures would, or even could, have any impact on a person, let alone how the cards could so consistently show the difficulties that existed in my life. What weird magic was this? And why couldn't I see the trick? How could all 78 cards, no matter how I drew them, speak to me on such a personal level?

The answer was relatively simple: every card I pulled was the answer I sought at any given moment. The Thoth deck by Aleister Crowley and the fantastic artwork by Lady Frieda Harris spoke to me with profound eloquence and are the basis of the intuitive Tarot work within this book.

Each image speaks to a deeper part of the psyche in a language without words but impacts the subconscious level. Every card represents part of the greater Self in the journey along life's path, whether in the present, a past lesson learned, or a pattern that will repeat going forward.

It doesn't matter which cards are part of the spread—only that they appear now. Every card has a message, delivered regardless of when it shows up. Even though there are some cards I've never pulled, I'm deeply aware of their significance in the bigger picture. Knowing both the psychology and mystery of Tarot deepens the understanding of life.

The cards are not New Age. They are Old Age, which means ancient people of many cultures have used these symbols to explain the world around them for thousands of years. Tarot is not about divining the future but about accepting who you are in the present. Humans exist on four levels of consciousness: physical, mental, emotional, and spiritual. Examining these levels with each card brings profound personal revelations and enlightenment on the journey through life.

The three components of the book (Major, Minor & Royalty) are designed to explain the structure of the Tarot deck, give personal insight, bring a sense of the deeper self through symbols and self-meditation, and, ultimately, the ability to read for yourself and others.

Tarot is a psychological tool that delves into the unconscious, seeking existing answers. The revelation comes in seeing preexisting patterns and the choices made daily. I sincerely hope these pages guide you to understand the repetitions in your life.

This book is based on the Thoth (Crowley) Tarot deck, which can be as intimidating as it is rich in symbolic language, but it is not necessary to use that deck. The book can also benefit meditation without a deck by using the questions at the end of each card as a source for your journaling experience. Each page captures the essence of the archetypical language and speaks to the deeper unconscious self.

Use the archetypes as a tool for self-evaluation. The stories unfold, the choices presented, and the reader becomes aware of personal lessons that drive behavior. What one chooses to do with that information is up to that individual, but once an insight has surfaced, there is no return to an oblivious existence.

Each card's positive and negative sides are introduced in the text to gain unique insight and knowledge. The questions at the end of each card description are designed to invoke a thoughtful dialogue, encourage the discovery of new perceptions, and gather information to help guide decisions. To be whole, one must examine all aspects of the psyche.

Tarot is the voice of inner wisdom with multiple layers to consider while contemplating your life. Take your time, return to the cards with the most significant impact, and chart how the questions change as you evolve. It isn't necessary to have a background in Tarot or to have studied the symbols to benefit from the reflections on each card.

You may also use the questions as a personal meditation for journaling without the cards and as a focal point for group discussion.

Understanding Tarot is one part knowledge and three parts intuition. Understanding the actual meanings and intention of the author and artist of a deck is helpful, but allowing the Higher Self to speak to you in deep symbolic language is, by far, the more significant advantage.

Enjoy your voyage into a world rich with archetypical intentions to help you achieve self-fulfillment.

    Blessings from Ruth Souther

Dr. Ruth A. Souther

Tarot 101: Introduction to the Mysteries

Imagine a deck of standard playing cards that range from the Ace to the King in each of the four suits. The Minor Arcana and the Royalty represent this layout: Ace through King in typical Tarot decks and Ace through Queen in the Thoth Tarot deck.

The suits in most Tarot designs are based on the Rider-Waite-Smith deck. The suits are represented by Wands/Staffs, Swords, Cups, and Disks/Pentacles.

Many other Tarot designs incorporate these energies in different patterns (Apprentice, Mage, Seer, Master, etc., and some version of the four suits). Still, it is best to look at those particular decks' instructions to understand the artwork's ideology.

There are ways to incorporate the information in this book with those different analogies. The basic Royalty or Court cards and how they interact with the rest of the deck are similar yet listed in a way suited to that particular deck.

We begin to see the connection between the suits of Wands, Swords, Disks, and Cups. So, then, how is the Royalty connected to the Major Archetypes? How do they all work together?

The **Major Arcana** is the overriding, archetypical energy that collects in your lifetime – the significant lessons and experiences you draw from to make decisions. The **Minor Arcana** becomes the stumbling block in your path to slow down your progress.

They also can be the necessary support to push you to achieve. Once you understand, the block will dissolve, the help will surface, and you will focus on the next obstacle, gaining momentum.

The following is a brief description of the Major and Minor Arcana.

ARCANA = WISDOM (Major/Minor)

The **Major Arcana** are 22 larger-than-life lessons and experiences that align you with your destiny. They tell the story of being human and bring into focus the moments when your higher consciousness points to the opportunities that propel you forward when Universal wisdom is readily available to assist you with important decisions.

In the Thoth (Crowley) deck, the **Major Arcana** is depicted as mythical, eclectic, and stylized versions of a human figure rather than a human being, as in the Rider-Waite-Smith and most other decks.

The Heart Of Tarot

The purpose is to allow an archetypical energy to flow from the image, to lift the reader from the confines of physical life to an elevated vibration and connection with the collective mind.

The **Major Arcana** unfolds in three stages: inner-personal work, inter-personal relationships, and trans-personal connections. Think of a child who first learns to talk, walk, and be aware of the surroundings (inner-personal).

The child grows into a young adult, defining who and what life and love are about (interpersonal). Finally, they become an elder who has accrued so much experience and wisdom that the details become insignificant as spiritual truth emerges (trans-personal).

The **Major Arcana** starts with The Fool (Conception) and flows to The Universe (Completion). You are then presented with the Immortal Portal. This end that becomes the beginning allows choice: you throw yourself through to conception to start all over again. Or you don't because there are lessons still to learn.

Each cycle is metaphoric yet felt in all aspects of Self: Mind, Body, Heart, and Spirit. Then, you turn to the **Minor Arcana** to clarify the finer points, the misunderstandings, and the repeated lessons, some more pleasant than others. To evolve, you must resolve the issues through determined work.

The **Minor Arcana** consists of 40 messages that play over and over daily until you get the significance of the lesson. Sometimes, it takes great effort to open your eyes and see the pattern that is the root cause behind the problem.

In the Thoth (Crowley) deck, the **Minor Arcana** is depicted strictly with the symbols from the elements they represent and contains no human figures. Other decks, like the Rider-Waite-Smith and most others, show human beings as the focus.

The Crowley/Coleman-Smith interpretation unleashes a broader range of motion, emotion, thought, and creativity than the mere illustration of people portraying an activity. For example, a blonde man will appear and take your money, or a tall, dark woman will enter your life as a lover.

The **Minor Arcana** has four categories: Air, Fire, Water, and Earth that reflect the elements of the natural world. There are ten cards per suit, Ace—10

- Air is the mental aspect of being human and is your thoughts, voice, and means of communication.
- Fire is the authentic aspect of being human and is your creativity, instincts, and beliefs.
- Water is the emotional aspect of being human and is your feelings, passion, and response.

- Earth is the physical aspect of being human and is your body, presence, and nature.

There is, of course, so much more to these daily obstacles, successes, and expressions of life, but your intuitive Self makes the difference.

Rather than trying to analyze each symbol appearing in your deck or reading books that define the symbols according to someone's research, accept what you already know when you look at the card images.

At first glance, one point jumps out: color, an odd shape, a symbol that speaks to you, or even the overall impression or feeling you get when you look at the card. Trust yourself to know what you see is what you need to further your path of self-knowledge and healing.

The Heart Of Tarot

What, exactly, is an Archetype?

It is the original pattern or model from which all things of the same kind are copied or on which they are based: a model or first form, a prototype.

In Jungian psychology, an archetype is a collectively inherited unconscious idea, pattern of thought, image, etc, that is universally present in all individual psyches.
   (Source: Dictionary.com)

The following pages are examples of how archetypes, or patterns, exist in our personal lives, as witnessed by the characters within the Major Arcana.

Archetypes exist everywhere in our lives, modeling behaviors that impact us unconsciously. Some of these archetypes are easy to see, as in teacher, athlete, healer, politician, or comedian. Archetypes come in many forms.

These Archetypes express both positive and negative energy. The purpose is to serve as an essential guide and illustrate how to grow and evolve in human form.

Using the following questions, either through a card draw or journaling, you will discover an added layer of how the whole deck engages the four elements of air, earth, fire, and water. Each element represents a part of the human condition and helps to overcome the issues that threaten to slow or even stop your progress.

It is especially true if you are beginning to learn Tarot. The symbols, colors, archetypes, elements, and astrological influences add additional layers to shift your awareness. Allow your instincts to interpret what you see, and then go with your first thought or feeling. I believe reading cards is 75% intuition and 25% intellectual input.

The Heart of Tarot has three sections:

The <u>Major Arcana</u> (22 Archetypes) tells a story from the Fool (0) to the Universe (21). These are the fundamental lessons of life and indicate the truth as expressed by the unconscious. Each meditation for the Major Arcana reflects on the state of the Higher Self and the conduit of wisdom waiting to open.

An additional note—if you need more information or if a particular image does not resonate, you may want to draw an extra card to help with the process. These cards give clarity and insight and offer ways to work out the process of inner growth.

The Card of Protection is included in the Major Arcana section and is only found in the Thoth deck. There was a period when the deck was without the Card of Protection, but restored in the newer versions. Other decks may have changed the names of the archetypes represented in the Major Arcana, but the fundamental meaning of each remains the same. Cross-referencing the information from your deck will help align the differences.

The Minor Arcana (4 Elemental Suits) begins with the Aces, the purest essence of the element, and progresses to the Tens, which are the most difficult. All the cards present life-altering questions that pursue us in life. You will most likely be drawn (or resistant) to specific suits. These energies will appear to be the strongest in your life and, therefore, deserve a closer examination, including the more negative aspects of the card.

The temptation is to ignore the lessons presented, but these energies are the very ones that help the most to work through the levels. Each layer will take you deeper into the issue, like peeling an onion. What may, at first, appear to be the truth revealed often turns out to be just one more step forward to resolve the conflicts in your life. Keep an open mind to the physical, emotional, mental, and spiritual evolution offered with the symbols of the cards.

The Thoth Minor Arcana suits are **Wands (Fire)**, **Swords (Air)**, **Disks (Earth)**, and **Cups (Water)**. Other decks may have shifted the names, but the core meanings are the same across the board.

Fire is your authentic self—it is how you identify your morals. **Air** is your communication process—how you convey your truth. **Earth** is your physical presence in the world—how you define your boundaries. **Water** is your emotional state—how you express your feelings. These are the fundamental and often repeated lessons of life faced daily.

The Royalty (16 Challenge Cards) section represents the inspiration for moving through the lessons presented by the other cards. How do you deal with emotional dilemmas? How do you use critical thought to work through issues? How do you reflect your authentic self to the world?

How do you embody your values and maintain a physical presence? The Thoth Royalty depicts the Princess, Prince, Knight, and Queen. Many other decks follow the Rider-Waite Smith lineage of Page, Knight, Queen, and King. Some decks have changed the names altogether, but each carries the heart of the royal challenge.

The Princess is the Inspiration—she takes the first step. The Prince is the Architect—he moves inspiration into a design. The Knight is the Producer—he takes the design and builds it. The Queen is the Successor—she assesses the design, approves the project, and takes ownership. These cards represent the opportunity to overcome the difficulties you face.

You may find yourself driven, immersed, oblivious, or even lost within the energies of these cards. They represent the symbolic journey through life's ups and downs. The questions after each card are a path to self-discovery. Each page of this book has five critical words at the top for a snapshot into the energy of that particular card.

At the end of each section—Major, Minor, Royalty—is a quick reference grid with all the words associated with each card. As you read through each list, notice the terms build on each other and tell a story. It is the human condition as it unfolds, embraces, and mystifies with the beauty of our soul growth.

For further explanation of the symbols within the Thoth deck, I recommend *The Tarot Handbook* by Angeles Arrien. The wisdom within those pages has served me well. Insight, courage, strength, and the determination to move forward in the evolution of the soul are possible through the pages of this book.

Take time and enjoy the journey!

Dr. Ruth A. Souther

Tarot is a reflection of the human condition

The Heart Of Tarot

THE MAJOR ARCANA

*the mysteries of evolving
human life
as seen through the eyes of
archetypical energy*

Dr. Ruth A. Souther

The Quest: Discovering Self

Inner-personal Awareness is the development of self-awareness to become fully conscious.

0 Fool	–	Conception (birth)
1 Magician	=	Self (identity)
2 Priestess	=	Intuition (interaction)
3 Empress	=	Nature (need)
4 Emperor	=	Authority (boundaries)
5 Hierophant	=	Society (rules)
6 Lovers	=	Relationships (choices)
7 Charioteer	=	Path (control)

Inter-personal Growth evolves from innocence to involvement through a maturing perspective.

8 Adjustment	=	Truth (alignment)
9 Hermit	=	Solitude (quest)
10 Wheel of Fortune	=	Change (conflict)
11 Lust	=	Integration (power)
12 Hanged One	=	Restriction (perspective)
13 Death	=	Transformation (actualization)
14 Art	=	Balance (assimilation)

Tran-personal Choice establishes a relationship with society and brings peace and wisdom through understanding the higher self.

15 Devil	=	Temptation (bondage)
16 Tower	=	Upheaval (action)
17 Star	=	Acceptance (realization)
18 Moon	=	Authenticity (obsession)
19 Sun	=	Clarity (determination)
20 Aeon	=	Achievement (manifestation)
21 Universe	=	Wholeness (completion)

Tarot is the Inner Voice of Wisdom

Listen Well

Dr. Ruth A. Souther

0 - Fool	Innocence	Spontaneous	Fearless	Optimist	Uninhibited
1 - Magician	Communication	Flexibility	Resilient	Conscious	Dedicated
2 - Priestess	Independent	Intuitive	Balanced	Objectivity	Inner Wisdom
3 - Empress	Nurturing	Grounded	Fertile	Receptive	Creative
4 - Emperor	Security	Boundaries	Authority	Confident	Assertive
5 - Hierophant	Teacher	Apprentice	Ethical	Disciplined	Integrated
6 - Lovers	Relationships	Responsibility	Choices	Dualities	Oppositions
7 - Chariot	Self-Disciplined	Autonomous	Focused	Protected	Victorious
8 - Adjustment	Personal Truth	Perspective	Clarity	Alignment	Assimilation
9 - Hermit	Contemplation	Introspection	Solitude	Completion	Observation
10 - Wheel	Consequences	Recognition	Adaptation	Expansion	Abundance
11 - Lust	Courageous	Persevering	Sensual	Instinctual	Resourceful
12 - Hanged One	Suspension	Limitations	Transition	Surrender	Development
13 - Death	Transformation	Foundations	Severance	Release	Regeneration
14 - Art	Consolidation	Impartial	Positive	Enthusiasm	Compatibility
15 - Devil	Mischievous	Innovative	Bondage	Confusion	Obsessive
16 - Tower	Upheaval	Liberation	Change	Insights	Awakening
17 - Star	Self-Reliant	Regeneration	Inspiration	Renewal	Originality
18 - Moon	Authentic	Deception	Mysterious	Sensitive	Meditative
19 - Sun	Enlightened	Conscious	Determined	Successful	Motivated
20 - Aeon	Evolution	Fulfillment	Stability	Harmony	Wisdom
21 – Universe	Completion	Freedom	Wholeness	Maturity	Valiant
Protection	Safety	Guardian	Security	Boundaries	Fundamental

The Heart Of Tarot

0 - THE FOOL

**INNOCENT
UNINHIBITED
SPONTANEOUS
OPTIMISTIC
FEARLESS**

Astrology Note: Uranus – the development of individuality

The Fool represents a state of consciousness experienced before birth and after death. An **innocent** heart has no expectations, stands in a state of suspended animation, and waits to leap into the next opportunity. The Fool is the ability to develop individual expression.

You begin as pure spirit, the life force of **uninhibited** and **spontaneous** thought, in a position to float and dream as the energetic essence of who you truly are. There is no awareness of what you will become. That knowledge does not yet exist.

You are ready to enter a physical body with courage, wonder, and great anticipation. Like stepping off the proverbial cliff, you have no apprehension of what is to come, only excitement filled with creative expression waiting to begin. You enter life with an **optimistic** outlook, free of all cares and worries, desiring to see what wonders this incarnation will bring.

The Fool's shadow holds the possibility of becoming inhibited and unable to allow any change to occur because of fear. Where the Fool would typically embrace a new idea with optimism, you might become rigid and unavailable, playing far inside your limitations rather than taking a risk.

Where the Fool trusts the instinctual self and is ready to take a leap of faith, you might become suspicious and restless, unable to commit to any task or purpose. You could be set adrift in many ways with no goal in your line of sight. Disillusion brings frustration, which often leads to irresponsible behavior. You may be unable to go forward, caught in a trap of your making.

The Fool is fearless. Residing within the spirit of Self is an abiding sense of trust in the significant patterns of life. Willing to take that leap of faith, the Fool steps into the physical world and is ready for change.

Dr. Ruth A. Souther

Questions from the Fool:

- What are you ready to birth?

- What fear keeps you from moving forward?

- How do you get past this limitation?

- What represents fearlessness as you change?

- What allows you to take a leap of faith

The Heart Of Tarot

1 - THE MAGICIAN

INDIVIDUAL
RESILIENT
FLEXIBLE
CONSCIOUS
DEDICATED

Astrology Note: Mercury – the recognition of independent thought

The Magician represents clear communication as a tool to express distinctive ideas and views. Once in physical form, an identity starts to take shape, and through identity, the art of being an **individual**. The Magician is the ability to recognize independent thought.

Immediately upon finding yourself present in the world, you yearn to connect with others. Such thought is an instinctive reaction. It is where you begin to mold the **resilient**, **flexible** self you are to become and discover the inherent human condition that desires company. However, before an exchange can occur, you must first be conscious of yourself and understand what motivates action.

It would be best to initiate an internal dialogue that communes with your deepest Self to discover the magic within your soul before you can extend your voice outward. You must know your gifts before sharing them with the greater world. Being **dedicated** to the work most important to you will result in the ability to share your magic with others.

The Magician's shadow may isolate you and deprive you of the desire to communicate your thoughts and ideas. You may find you can scarcely voice the reasons to yourself, let alone explain why you are stuck externally. Results often place blame on others for your inabilities. The magic turns sour and holds no mystery, so you stop trying.

Your intentions are not clear. You may not follow through with the most minor step towards attaining your goal. Ideas, once important, fade into the background when unhappiness becomes overwhelming. You may then become dedicated to nothing and go nowhere. Your identity becomes a mere shadow if you lose sight of yourself.

The Magician listens carefully to the inner dialog and notes the essential thoughts to convey to others. The message that follows is clear and concise.

Dr. Ruth A. Souther

Questions from the Magician:

- What hidden voice waits to speak to you?

- What stops you from listening to new ideas?

- How do you regain the magic in your life?

- What motivates you to share your gifts?

- How will you share your gifts in the future?

The Heart Of Tarot

2 - THE PRIESTESS

**INTUITION
INDEPENDENCE
RESOURCEFUL
OBJECTIVE
EXPERIENCED**

Astrology Note: Moon – the ability to respond emotionally

The Priestess represents **intuition** and a profound sense of self-trust while maintaining the urgent demand for a balance between the internal and external worlds. The Priestess is the ability to respond emotionally to a logical thought.

Your conscious and subconscious physical well-being and spiritual health depend on the ability to take your internal dialogue and compare it to the external landscape. To have a healthy balance, you must discover the point of interaction between what is logically known and what you emotionally feel.

From this place, you discover your originality and the need to be **independent**. You access your wisdom to evaluate situations and find **resourceful** ways to resolve problems. **Objective** behavior comes from a place of self-reliance and good judgment as you distance yourself from the chaos around you. The Priestess is the present. She stands between the past and future timelines, offering perspective and insight into the many issues of your life.

The Priestess' shadow tends to withdraw when chaos becomes unbearable. Your inclination may be to turn away from and ignore possible solutions to maintain your balance. Sometimes, you might be perceived as cold, uncaring, superficial, and insincere because your emotions are raw and out of control.

You will not allow your weaknesses to show. Your control and misplaced determination may cause another layer of confusion, adding to your frustration. Although detachment appears to resolve the issue, this action can pull you further from the state of peace you desire.

The Priestess honors the instinctual Self and listens to the voice of wisdom from an experienced and intuitive position. The duality becomes a place of personal power, and truth is the guiding light to objectivity.

Dr. Ruth A. Souther

Questions from the Priestess:

- **What does your intuition tell you?**

- **What truth do you turn away from?**

- **How do you maintain your perspective?**

- **How do you find objectivity in the chaos?**

- **What connects you to the mysteries of life?**

The Heart Of Tarot

3 - THE EMPRESS

NURTURING
GROUNDED
FERTILE
RECEPTIVE
CREATIVE

Astrology Note: Venus – the development of emotional bonds

The Empress represents the **nurturing** capacity to give and receive love while remaining **grounded** in the abundance of self-confidence and personal respect. The Empress is the ability to develop emotional bonds and share profound prosperity with others. She is the archetypical mother figure who understands the natural world's cycles.

You are prepared to share your **fertile** wealth with the world for the greater good. You are the epitome of beauty and creative power, symbolizing nature at the deepest level. You discover the ability to balance a trusting heart with the fierce knowledge of primal protection.

You represent the infinite Yin with your **receptive** and **creative** energy and the capacity to heal yourself. With this belief in personal growth, you must reach out to others and offer comfort and support. Your greatest gift is permitting yourself to evolve emotionally to a higher sense of purpose in life.

The Empress's shadow may create depression, leading to self-indulgence, extravagance, and overspending from both the emotional and physical levels. If you find yourself out of balance with the natural cycles of your life, you may become disempowered, rejecting love and withdrawing support from those around you.

Feelings of uselessness compound the excesses rather than allowing you to seek harmony, good health, and the return of creativity. Your receptivity may shut down as your vanity becomes focused on selfish desires, which prevents developing emotional bonds with others.

The Empress first nurtures from within as a devoted mother figure, bringing the fertile opportunity to receive love from others. With channels wide open, healthy self-empowerment and honest love are achievable.

Dr. Ruth A. Souther

Questions from the Empress:

- What blocks you from emotional truth?

- What symbolizes disempowerment?

- How do you remain grounded and balanced?

- How are you open to giving and receiving love?

- How do you regain your identity?

The Heart Of Tarot

4 - THE EMPEROR

**AUTHORITY
BOUNDARIES
SECURITY
CONFIDENCE
GUIDANCE**

Astrology Note: Aries – the development of willpower

The Emperor represents **authority**, leadership, and the capacity to place **boundaries** around everything necessary for survival. The Emperor is the ability to develop willpower and strength to carry on in the face of great adversity.

Security is of the utmost importance to you. As you strive to make your world stable, solid, and safe for yourself and all others within your realm, you discover **confidence** is rooted in logical thought. You follow your beliefs and ideals and keep a curious and open mind.

You allow yourself to evolve with new ideas while defending what already exists. One of your gifts is to be a builder of cities and society. Once you recognize your power and understand you are the foundation, you begin to see how your interaction with others is affected. You discover that enlightened **guidance** allows you to serve others well and that your authority serves a higher Self.

The Emperor's shadow tends toward tyranny, leading to attitudes of self-righteousness followed by ineffectual leadership. Your role is to guide and protect, but focusing only on your power may make you selfish and arrogant. The foundation you seek to build becomes riddled with decay and poor quality. Eventually, all hope is lost, and the structure you worked so hard on is abandoned.

Your loss of control undermines your authority. When your reality is confused with false pride, your boundaries are compromised. The Emperor becomes overly critical and judgmental, and you are poorly served.

The Emperor maintains authority while creating stability for others. Completely aware of the difference between rigid control and empowered leadership, the Emperor acts with honor and compassion while building foundations.

Dr. Ruth A. Souther

Questions from the Emperor:

- **What boundaries need protection?**

- **How do you recognize self-inflicted tyranny?**

- **When has your authority been undermined?**

- **What is your guidance for a new foundation?**

- **How do you reclaim your power?**

The Heart Of Tarot

5 - THE HIEROPHANT

**TEACHER
APPRENTICE
ETHICAL
DISCIPLINED
INTEGRATES**

Astrology Note: Taurus – the development of conscience

The Hierophant represents the dichotomy between **teacher** and **apprentice**, constantly integrating what is known with the lessons continuously presented. The Hierophant is the development of a higher conscience and is the bridge between knowledge and understanding.

You are aware life is constant and ever-changing and will never happen again the same way. Embrace every experience as an opportunity to learn something new. You realize what you have to offer to society represents self-made rules, and rules are to be examined and questioned rather than mindlessly followed.

You are highly **ethical** and **disciplined**, reaching beyond yourself to the divine Universe and yet keeping your feet secure and grounded on the Earth. You discover how flexible and innovative your views can be as you contemplate heaven, earth, and all that is connected. By offering yourself as the conduit, you create infinite awareness between the conscious and unconscious Self.

The Hierophant's shadow can become rigid and dogmatic in your views. You can easily succumb to your power trip and become unethical and immoral. Ultimately, you may be the outsider because of aggressive behavior and lack of respect for authority.

You might cling to self-imposed rules and refuse to see your self-abuse patterns, undermining the ideal you strive to achieve. No longer an open channel, you could become confused and lose sight of your convictions. Your conscience no longer functions at a higher level of awareness but blindly turns toward hypocritical thought and action.

***The Hierophant integrates** new knowledge with old and constantly re-evaluates life. Steadfastly adhering to a higher Self and a pattern of ethical behavior brings deep satisfaction.*

Dr. Ruth A. Souther

Questions from the Hierophant:

- **What self-imposed rule should you question?**

- How do you avoid being rigid and dogmatic?

- How do you integrate wisdom with behavior?

- How do you access higher consciousness?

- How do you become the bridge to change?

The Heart Of Tarot

6 - THE LOVERS

RELATIONSHIPS
DUALITIES
RESPONSIBILITY
CHOICES
DECISIONS

Astrology Note: Gemini – the development of communication

The Lovers represent **relationships**. Reconnecting the lost bond between the external masculine voice and the internal feminine wisdom brings emotional unity with the Higher Self. The Lovers is the development of external communication while facing life's choices with courage.

Be reminded of each individual's **dualities** and the different aspects of responsibility experienced in life. Because relationships are varied and complex, the Lovers also represent the **choices** you make and the paths you choose to follow. You must remember those principles that have heart and give meaning to your life rather than the more shallow and straightforward ways that could lead to unhappiness.

You have the gift of integration as you bring together conflicting ideas while instilling inner peace during challenging **decisions**. You can achieve this through communication with heartfelt, intuitive, intellectual, and balanced interactions of the spoken word. Verbalize your options, dissect the resolutions, and review your direction before you take action.

The Lovers' shadow may suppress individuality and freedom of choice. There can be issues around taking responsibility for actions, which undermines relationships and creates disagreements. The dispute stems from a lack of internal communication, as you may argue fiercely with yourself about the dualities.

Externally, you may refuse to take other opinions or options under consideration. Issues of indecision, guilt, and confusion add to the exchange layers, resulting in a separation from reality and an ultimate self-imposed isolation.

The Lovers face many paths and many choices through their relationship with the Self and the external world. The responsibility is to see the dualities presented, combine the thoughts, and then communicate the ideas into a workable solution.

Dr. Ruth A. Souther

Questions from the Lovers:

- What relationship undermines self-worth?

- How do you integrate opposing forces and bring emotional peace?

- Where are the dualities that confuse your life?

- How do you communicate with heartfelt, balanced opinions?

- How do you evaluate your choices?

The Heart Of Tarot

7 - THE CHARIOT

**FOCUSED
CONFIDENT
PROTECTED
CHAMPION
VICTORIOUS**

Astrology Note: Cancer—the development of survival tactics

The Chariot represents the change from a place of **focused** and **confident** maturity with the instinct to survive on all four levels of being human - physical, emotional, mental, and spiritual. The Chariot is the ability to develop survival tactics in the external world.

Your bravery is called into question as you maintain your struggle to be independent while retaining the motivation to move forward. You are ready for battle, **protected** by the armor of strategy, prepared to commit if the need arises, yet you have not taken up weapons. Faced with a choice, you either ride into battle or withdraw and concede.

Either way requires an action of some sort. You survive by choosing when you will fight and when you will take flight. You must exert great courage to become the **champion**, realizing that victory is internal. Adapting to the moment is necessary if you are ready to take action. All things grow and evolve just as you grow; this knowledge forces an assessment of what needs to change in your life. You must find the correct course of action to further your expansion.

The Chariot's shadow tends to be overconfident, which creates rash and reckless behavior. Rather than moving with deliberate self-discipline, you may become agitated when things are too slow, or events do not reconcile quickly enough. You may get out of control with an inflated ego and find yourself intimidating others to get what you want.

As your energy becomes scattered, you may become distracted from your goals and achieve little but frustration and anger at your invisibility. Survival depends upon your perception and ability to change and grow with each lesson.

*The Charioteer has chosen a path and moves forward with purpose. The Chariot arrives **victorious** by being deliberate with any action, protected by the armor of courage, and seeking to survive with conscientious direction.*

Questions from the Charioteer:

- When has overconfidence undermined your choices?

- What gives you the strength to listen to your instincts?

- Where do you find yourself victorious through self-confidence?

- How do you take independent action?

- How can you focus your intentions?

The Heart Of Tarot

8 - ADJUSTMENT

**PERSPECTIVE
CLARITY
PERSONAL TRUTH
ALIGNMENT
ASSIMILATE**

Astrology Note: Libra – the reconciliation of opposites

Adjustment represents finding balance during turmoil while at the same time seeking the principles of negotiation and truth. Adjustment is the ability to find reconciliation and harmony in opposing views. Stand in the present rather than what is past or what might be the future. You gain insight into your projections by viewing the current situation.

To make sense of the chaos, you must find **perspective**. You intend to bring more clarity, stability, and simplicity into your life through this process. This is the time to acknowledge your **personal truth** and the ideas and thoughts that support who you are now rather than those opinions and beliefs that no longer serve.

You must clear out the clutter from your mind and view existing circumstances honestly. You can gain new perceptions of old situations by finding the correct alignment. You can **assimilate** the lessons of the past, the events of the present, and the possibilities of the future. From this place of integrity, you become centered and discover the harmony you so desperately seek.

Adjustment's shadow likes to over-analyze and dissect every word, thought, and idea until you become incapable of any perspective. Plagued with indecision, overwhelmed by information, you forget why you questioned yourself.

You may lose sight of your authenticity and fall back on old patterns as you cling to old ideals. You can become harshly critical of both yourself and everyone around you. This may result in nothing learned from these past lessons. You may see no connection in the present and view the future with pain and confusion.

Adjustment seeks balance and growth around core principles but never forgets that understanding the past brings insight into the future. Finding harmony with the higher Self brings stability to both the internal and external landscapes.

Questions from Adjustment:

- What new perspective is waiting?

- Where is the balance between old and new ideas?

- When have you lost sight of your authenticity?

- What truth brings harmony into your life?

- How do you stay focused and in the present?

The Heart Of Tarot

9 - THE HERMIT

CONTEMPLATION
INTROSPECTION
COMPLETION
SOLITUDE
OBSERVATION

Astrology Note: Virgo—the search for purpose

The Hermit represents **contemplation, introspection,** and **completion** at the junction most critical to an adult presence in the world. Taking light into the darkest corners of life gives the opportunity to reveal hidden truths. The Hermit has the ability to search for a higher purpose in life's complicated patterns.

You discover the need to conclude unfinished business and reorganize and evaluate your path. Your desire for **solitude** causes you to retreat from civilization. You take time to examine and weigh that which has been and all that will ever be. You are driven to realign around the higher Self, even if this means abandoning the present quest.

Your mission is to transcend the errors of the past and redefine yourself in a new, positive, and powerful light. You grow quiet and observe every detail. You listen to the beat of your own heart. You reassess your strengths and weaknesses as you learn to follow your instincts by allowing the cycle of growth to complete.

The Hermit's shadow tends to become so tied to this newfound introspective self that you may become a recluse, rejecting all socialization. You enjoy the sense of freedom that comes with lighting your path so much that you may fail to see how you push others away.

The sense of detachment grows as your point of reflection becomes skewed, and the lovely solitary path becomes a lonely, bitter experience. The seclusion is a time of healing, a place to rest and become centered. Instead, if you stay there too long, you risk building permanent living quarters that deny the joy of life with others.

*The Hermit requires privacy to contemplate life and conclude unfinished business but never forgets the path will eventually lead out of the forest and back to the city lights. Powerful skills of **observation** bring sincere enlightenment.*

Questions from the Hermit:

- What represents unfinished business in life?

- What current goal should be reconsidered?

- How do you release past regrets?

- Where do you find strength and guidance?

- How do you find your way out of confusion?

The Heart Of Tarot

10 - FORTUNE

ABUNDANCE
EXPANSION
RECOGNITION
CONSEQUENCES
ADAPTATION

Astrology Note: Jupiter – the expansion of confidence

Fortune represents prosperity and personal growth if allowed to go with the flow, change, and adapt to evolving needs. The Wheel of Fortune is the ability to expand confidently, knowing each decision is a move forward.

You can handle conflict from a place of observation in the center of the Wheel rather than clinging for dear life on the edge as Fortune relentlessly cycles around and around. You are reminded of the prosperity and **abundance** waiting for you. If you gain control of your life and reject the idea of controversy, you will find your way toward progress and development. You recognize the truth of what goes up must come down.

For every **expansion,** there will also be a contraction. The **recognition** of old patterns as they occur is critical to understanding the **consequences** of your actions. You can accommodate life as it happens and adjust constantly to stay on a happy, even keel.

Fortune's shadow wants to whirl you about like a carnival ride, spinning so fast you lose control and do not realize which direction you face. Perhaps you will get stuck at the halfway mark. Maybe you will find yourself in limbo, out of control, and miserably unhappy at the mercy of others, particularly if you constantly react rather than take command of your life.

Succumbing to the exploitation surrounding you may bring more frustration and delays in your personal growth. You must find the confidence to step out of old patterns and make changes toward positive personal development.

*Fortune discovers that resistance to change is futile. Finding a place in the center of the Wheel provides a sense of peace and harmony and allows the higher Self to focus on personal enrichment rather than chaos. **Adaptation** is the key to success in negotiating life's rocky road.*

Dr. Ruth A. Souther

Questions from Fortune:

- **How do you handle the conflicts in your life?**

- **Where have you lost control?**

- **What provides confidence?**

- **What change brings positive growth?**

- **How do you survive the changes in your life?**

The Heart Of Tarot

11 - LUST

**COURAGEOUS
PERSISTENT
CREATIVE
INSTINCTUAL
SENSUAL**

Astrology Note: Leo – the capacity for physical expression

Lust represents personal power and the strength to communicate creativity and express the joy found within outwardly. Lust is the ability to find bliss in adversity and the thrill of accepting a new challenge or overcoming an old pattern that brings new confidence.

You discover an inherent faith in yourself and a **courageous** spark that drives you to be **persistent** in pursuing personal happiness. To find your power, you must first find your **creative** life force, that piece of yourself that radiates from the beauty within.

You must listen to the cadence of your **instinctual** nature and know that to transform, you must love and trust the inner beast of **sensual** self-expression. You become emotionally and physically balanced, a mirror image of harmony and enthusiasm that propels you passionately toward new horizons. You discover the capacity for physical articulation is steeped in spiritual freedom.

Lust's shadow tends to be overly daring and bold as you misjudge your strength. You are at the crossroads of an understanding with your innate self. You are tempted to miscalculate your ability to handle problems, which could lead to a severe collapse of faith.

You may become overwhelmed by things outside your control, which leads to questioning your personal goals. These questions could undermine the passion with which you seek new ideas and cause you to give up, withdraw, or even become disinterested in the possibilities.

Lust brings a rejuvenated sense of Self, a path of rediscovery, and faith in personal talents. Fiercely guard the right to choose which direction to take, but remember to balance the emotional and physical aspects.

Questions from Lust:

- What is your ability to handle issues?

- Where have you undermined creativity?

- How do you discover your empowerment?

- What hidden talent is waiting to be discovered?

- How do you release the martyr and claim your potential?

12 - THE HANGED MAN

SUSPENSION
PERCEPTIONS
SURRENDER
DEVELOPMENT
TRANSITION

Astrology Note: Neptune – the insight of perception

The Hanged Man represents the recognition of repetitive patterns restricting growth. Life often provides a state of **suspension** when an entirely new perspective is necessary to get past self-imposed points of view. The Hanged Man is the ability to gain insight into **perceptions** not based on physical impressions.

When you **surrender** to the moment and ponder what blocks you from going forward, you see many more options, solutions, and opportunities to consider than those currently invested. You remember your hang-ups prevent evolution and growth.

Developing new thoughts and ideas is critical as you search for a different approach to your problems. You must listen to your inner voice and the intuitive Self that sees beyond the physical reality into the layers of emotion, thought, and spirit.

The Hanged Man's shadow is often frustrated by this time of deep thought and often refuses to slow down. You might rush headlong into decisions that can cause regret while choosing to ignore the signs even as you crash into them. Should you decide not to pay attention and heed the warnings, you could march directly into martyrdom and sacrifice everything because of a single notion.

You may discover how to listen to the instinctual self while quieting the mind, heart, and body, but only temporarily. Rather than shifting into a period of isolation and loneliness, use this moment to suspend judgment.

The Hanged Man recognizes limiting behavior and adjusts perspective. Do not anticipate the outcome and be invested in the actions or reactions of others. Clear away the debris and focus on making the transition *between past and future goals.*

Dr. Ruth A. Souther

Questions from the Hanged Man:

- What behavior restricts your move forward?

- When have you rushed into harmful action?

- How do you find a different approach to old problems?

- What new and insightful perspective is waiting to be discovered?

- How does logic support you with decisions?

The Heart Of Tarot

13 - DEATH

TRANSFORMATION
FOUNDATION
RELEASE
OBJECTIVITY
REBIRTH

Astrology Note: Scorpio - the intensity of awareness

Death represents the **transformation** of old pain into new beginnings. After defining the limitations that prevent action, Death takes one step further and strips away all deception to reveal the bare bones of a solid **foundation**. Death is the ability to become intensely aware of patterns that no longer serve growth.

You have the strength to sever the ties to the old identity that binds you and **release** those no longer functional patterns. Much like a snake shedding its skin or the Phoenix rising from the ashes of its old self, you reach for an expanded consciousness and emerge reborn into a new existence.

You discover detachment is a form of **objectivity**, and suddenly, those issues that were so important are not important now. You begin to actualize, or make real, the changes necessary to start a new way of life. You discover the art of regeneration. You rebuild. You create a new structure and a stable and secure foundation.

Death's shadow can be resistant to change. The intensity of prolonged pain and distress may be present if you turn away from the reality that something needs to end. It may be a relationship, a thought process, a cherished idea, or many other possibilities. You might refuse to accept these moments of redefinition and reject the opportunity to grow and expand out of paralyzing fear.

What would happen if everything transformed? What if you let go of those things that are no longer valid? Is the grief attached to known pain better than the fear of the unknown? Find the courage to reach beyond self-imposed limitations into new possibilities by facing the mysterious yet exciting change within your grasp.

*Death severs the ties to old patterns and offers the chance for the higher Self to **rebirth** into a new reality. To survive, it is necessary to actualize change at the most primal level of existence.*

Questions from Death:

- What defines the bones of your existence?

- How do you cut the strings to an old identity?

- How do you accept the challenge to evolve?

- What new foundation do you need?

- What are you most afraid of?

The Heart Of Tarot

14 - ART

POSITIVE
INNOVATIVE
COMPATIBLE
CONSOLIDATION
ORIGINALITY

Astrology Note: Sagittarius - the gathering of information

Art represents balance and the adaption of all facets of being human into a **positive** whole being. After integrating the past with the present to create the future—a rebirth—it becomes apparent that these different aspects must blend to create something new. Art is the ability to gather information and develop it into an **innovative** concept.

It is necessary to honor your character's light and dark sides. You must unify the polar opposites that cause dissension within so that you can become a **compatible**, fully-developed human. You learn the Art of **consolidation**: bringing ideas, feelings, and physical needs into one being.

Like the ancient alchemists, you can turn base metal (your unconscious needs ignored) into gold (your conscious desires realized). The shadow side of the Self is just as important to acknowledge as the light side to comprehend the attitudes shaping your behavior. Your reflection becomes the moral compass and takes you deeper into authenticity.

Art's shadow is often intensely competitive and fans natural enthusiasm into an uncontrollable ego. There could be an impractical side throwing caution to the wind to achieve goals despite any concerns that might surface.

If you embrace this recklessness rather than remaining impartial to success just for success' sake, you will bring conflict and uncertainty into reality. Disharmony takes control, and you may not put a fresh spin on your life. Integration is necessary to find balance and authentic control over your own life.

*Art seeks to incorporate life's positive and negative lessons into a brand-new view, bringing **originality** and optimism to life. Patience becomes second nature in overcoming adversity and claiming the creative Self.*

Questions from Art:

- How do you recognize incompatibility?

- When has ego taken control?

- What guides you toward self-integration?

- How do you honor the light and dark sides?

- What alchemical process is waiting to happen?

The Heart Of Tarot

15 - *DEVIL*

GOOD HUMOR
BONDAGE
SACRED WOUNDS
TEMPTATION
MISCHIEVOUS

Astrology Note: Capricorn – the expression of integrity

The Devil represents the necessity to face problems with **good humor**, to actively see the comedy and, often, the absurdity of life. Looking at the trials and tribulations from the higher Self rather than from a base physical presence gives perspective. The Devil is the ability to express the integrity of genuine wit and intelligence when dealing with difficulties.

If you take the issues in your life too seriously, you can become mired in the swamp of your emotions and sink to the greatest depths of your fear. You may become oppressed and unable to move forward. Look closely at the things you are in **bondage** to—those **sacred wounds** you hold dearly and nurture for all the wrong reasons.

The **temptation** to wallow in real or imagined problems is so profound in human nature that a **mischievous** viewpoint can help pull away from the internal dialogue threatening your integrity. You are offered many choices to change, let go of the past, and evolve with courage into the unknown.

The Devil's shadow often obsesses over inconsequential details. Suppose you live in constant confusion, unable to discern positive from negative. In that case, you may become moralistic, preaching your attitudes and opinions as if yours is the only valid perspective.

You might hold tightly to your pain to avoid the truth, which creates a larger-than-life sacred wound that could become your sole identity. You might become more structured and rigid, which could develop limitations and frustrations. The result could be a loss of confidence, sense of humor, and everything you have worked so hard to maintain.

The Devil tends to take problems too seriously, creating a sense of repression. It is necessary to cultivate the desire to recognize the things that create bondage to be free of obsessive behavior. Laughter is a great healer.

Questions from the Devil:

- What are you in bondage to?

- Where have you lost your sense of humor?

- How do you let go of past mistakes?

- What choice will free you from oppression?

- What choice do you need to make?

The Heart Of Tarot

16 - TOWER

UPHEAVAL
CHANGE
LIBERATION
INSIGHT
CLEANSING

Astrology Note: Mars – the fortitude of courage

The Tower represents **upheaval** and **change**. It calls to the greater Self to tear down the walls, restore a sense of well-being, come out of isolation, and begin healing. The Tower is the ability to find the fortitude of courage deep inside, reject the obsessions, and reach for complete **liberation**.

Imagine you have just awakened from a long sleep during which you have become something other than your true self. You find you are locked in a tower of false ideals and expectations, a tower built brick by brick around you. The Tower is a protective mechanism rather than constructed to be a prison. You chose to isolate yourself, climb to the top of the Tower, and view the world from a place far removed from the chaos.

You are left void of emotions and unable to interact with others. Even though you recognize the things you take too seriously in life, you have done nothing to correct your path. It is time to act upon that **insight** or forever be trapped. Take action—dismantle the tower, walk away from the rubble, and liberate yourself once and for all from those things that do not serve you.

The Tower's shadow can lose sight of freedom because you cling to established patterns even when you know they do more harm than good. You may allow yourself to be oppressed and imprisoned out of fear. What if nothing is waiting for you? What if you fail?

What if you succeed? It is better to hole up inside your fortress and remain in exile than deal with reality. Inside the Tower, you can pretend that pain and anxiety do not exist. You do not have to face the crumbling infrastructure of your beliefs if you never let it see the sunlight.

The Tower is a reminder that change is good and upheaval is cleansing. Letting go of old structures that no longer contribute to the evolution of spirit is healthy and right. Life is a continuous revolution.

Dr. Ruth A. Souther

Questions from the Tower:

- What idea or pattern holds you hostage?

- Where do you find the courage to let go?

- What action brings down the walls of isolation?

- How do you climb out of the rubble and move on?

- What light leads you forward?

The Heart Of Tarot

17 - THE STAR

INSPIRATION
REGENERATION
RENEWAL
SELF-RELIANCE
AWAKENING

Astrology Note: Aquarius - the desire for freedom

The Star represents **inspiration** and spiritual **regeneration** in a state of radiant **renewal.** The energy is neither inflated nor deflated but in proper balance with an expressive nature. The Star is the desire for freedom from oppression and the light at the end of a dark tunnel.

Once the Tower has exploded, you are free. You are forced into the night and begin to smell the sweet scent of success in the flowering meadow beneath your feet. You are inspired as you notice how far your dreams will stretch when you look at the banner of brilliant stars overhead.

You are the conduit, the channel that opens to your authentic self. You see that freedom provides the base for **self-reliance** and the path to accepting yourself as you truly are. Your gift is the strength to reach up and allow the original creative force to flow from the higher Self, through your body, to the ground, where your dreams manifest in reality. It is **awakening** from a dream state and the beginning of earthly manifestation.

The Star's shadow tends to be overwhelmed by the pressure created by your desires. You may become disillusioned by the difficulty of bringing your dreams to life and may have even set unattainable goals that position you for failure. You may be enamored of false status or appearance and become short-sighted. You may lose focus and become lost.

You must remember you are not The Star, but rather the star, one of many hundreds of thousands that send out light and create the beauty of the heavens for all to enjoy.

The Star embraces personal confidence and renewal of spiritual Self-cleansed of past wounds, offering a new beginning to create a fresh identity that expresses future desires. Hope springs eternal, just as the heavens will forever shine on.

Questions from the Star:

- What unproductive pressure have you created?

- When have you become disillusioned?

- How do you find inspiration and spiritual regeneration?

- What idea allows you to accept yourself?

- What dream is waiting to manifest?

The Heart Of Tarot

18 – THE MOON

AUTHENTIC
DECEPTIVE
MYSTERIOUS
RESPONSIVE
SENSITIVE

Astrology Note: Pisces – the association of instincts

The Moon represents the **authentic** Self and mature choices by offering the commitment to authenticity as a valid and sustaining path to wholeness. The Moon is the ability to associate instincts with free will and the courage to lead.

You face the duality of your identity: the face put forth to the world and the face that hides within. Those personalities merge and split, creating the possibility of a **deceptive** and false picture. Just as you shift in the shadows of the dark Moon, you also appear in the light of the full Moon.

You change just like the phases reflected in the night sky. There is an impression of lunacy as the **mysterious** certainty of who you are flirts with your conscious mind. Obsessions and choices are made that do not necessarily mirror your authentic nature. If you remain **sensitive** to the call of these inner tides, you can indeed be responsive to your higher consciousness.

The Moon's shadow can be unstable and wildly fluctuate while trying to maintain outwardly calm. If you spend too much time between fantasy and reality, you may become bewildered, confused, and unable to evolve into the higher Self you want to become.

Sometimes, you will refuse to listen to the rational thought process that will keep you sane. However, you may jump into the void despite knowing it will do more harm than good. Be aware of the cycles as you pass through them, and understand that the many faces of the Moon will bring deep awareness.

The Moon seeks an authentic self and strives to unite the subconscious with the conscious to create inward peace and wholeness. Merging both aspects will bring genuine external expressions into harmony.

Questions from the Moon:

- What trickery lies in the way of creating wholeness?

- When have you denied your true path?

- How do you respond to higher guidance?

- How do you embrace and celebrate your duality?

- How do you receive messages from your intuition?

The Heart Of Tarot

19 – THE SUN

MOTIVATED
DETERMINED
CONSCIOUS
CELEBRATION
ENLIGHTENED

Astrology Note: Sun – the establishment of ego

The Sun represents **motivated** and **determined** action aligned with clarity and inspiration. The Sun is the establishment of ego and the ability to consciously determine the most favorable course of action for Self while rejecting the negative implications that would restrict creativity.

You find affirmation in being **conscious** of your choices and desire to succeed in your chosen field. You are instilled with a sense of humor and a feeling of light-hearted play as your worries and fears are exposed as nonessential. Your path is clearly illuminated as you venture into the future, discovering joy in everyday life as long as you do not allow yourself to be consumed by the needs of others.

You discover that partnership with boundaries can be a transformative experience—a physical and spiritual progression that instills trust in your process. You find you are not alone on your path. Every moment of life is a celebration.

The Sun's shadow has an indulgent nature, which can cloud your judgment and allow you to be taken advantage of by those who see you as weak. You agree to help because it is the nature of the Sun to be available to everyone. You find yourself offering too much, too often.

You become too involved and too tired to say no. Burnout is a real problem. When that happens, you may become angry and insincere. Misunderstandings become commonplace. You fully embrace the concept that the world cannot turn without you; you are everything to everyone. In that case, there is the chance your ego will become inflated and border on overbearing and manipulative.

The Sun provides comprehension and enlightened faith. Becoming fully aware of innate talents and the abundant gifts brought to the world while remaining humble and filled with laughter is the reward of an honored ego.

Dr. Ruth A. Souther

Questions from the Sun:

- When has your ego clouded good judgment?

- How have misunderstandings gotten in your way?

- What motivates you to be fully conscious?

- What brings joy and inspiration?

- How do you embrace your true Self?

The Heart Of Tarot

20 - AEON

**EVOLUTION
WISDOM
FULFILLMENT
HARMONY
STABILITY**

Astrology Note: Pluto – the recognition of integrity

The Aeon represents the call to a more meaningful existence. Once motivated by the Sun to grow and reach further than ever, the Aeon now points the way to achieve goals through the **evolution** of spirit. The Aeon is the ability to recognize the source of integrity and embrace spiritual awareness.

You feel the call of **wisdom** from your deeper Self in response to the true nature of the universe. You must accept the past to progress into a higher mindset. You need to find the synchronization that unites body, mind, heart, and spirit.

Only then will you be able to make essential changes in your life—real change—a clearer mind, a joyful heart, a creative spirit, and a healthy body. Use good judgment to bring **fulfillment** and a sense of peace to yourself. You are content in the knowledge that you have finally achieved a state of Nirvana—the perfect condition of **harmony** and stability.

The Aeon's shadow has an opposition to change. You may even know you are stagnating. You may understand that holding onto old ideals is causing life to disintegrate right before your eyes. You may refuse to acknowledge the need for transformation.

You can become overly critical of others questioning your ways and even become judgmental and narrow-minded with your lack of perspective. Focus is constricted, and the bigger picture is ignored. You may refuse to cooperate and stubbornly stick to your selfish patterns rather than take responsibility. In the end, you undermine yourself and accomplish nothing.

The Aeon is achieved through the evolution of spirit. Personal responsibility is accepted. Every action reacts—the tiniest notion may cause waves. Establishing stability in a chaotic world means transcending the highest realms of integrity.

Questions from the Aeon:

- When have you resisted the call to reinvent yourself?

- Where have you been judgmental and narrow-minded?

- How do you clear your mind and reach for real change?

- What gives you the purpose to manifest your higher Self?

- How do you establish stability?

The Heart Of Tarot

21 - UNIVERSE

WHOLENESS
COMPLETION
FREEDOM
MATURITY
EVOLVED

Astrology Note: Saturn – the realization of destiny

The Universe represents **wholeness** and unification. It is the portal through which each individual must step to defeat fear and find **completion** as an evolved soul. The Universe is the ability to transcend the physical and realize that destiny awaits.

Stepping through the portal takes great courage and a brave spirit, but once done, there is a sense of **freedom** beyond words. You attain a state of ecstasy from which you see how far you have come. You have risen above and beyond who you once were.

You have been freed from all your fears and can now complete your journey with celebration. The Universe is dynamic and magnetic, unifying the opposites that once pulled you in different directions. You can see where you have been and where you are going. The mystery is solved: you know yourself inside and out. You have reached **maturity**. You have **evolved** and grown into the archetypical pattern meant for you. You have become an adult.

The Universe's shadow often refuses to take that last step. You are paralyzed by fear of the unknown, which limits your opportunities. When you are restricted by panic, your confidence is shaken. You no longer trust your instincts to guide you on the correct path. After all your work to evolve, devastation awaits if you do not take that last leap of faith.

Your awareness is such that you may no longer blame imperfection on anyone else. You may find you are solely responsible for your action, or in this case, inaction. Depression may follow, and you are caught in a stifling, self-made situation.

The Universe completes the circle. Once the soul steps through the portal of its greatest fears, it becomes all it is meant to be. The triumph is hard-won and well-deserved. Take time to celebrate and prepare for the next phase of your journey through life. The higher Self has achieved evolution.

Dr. Ruth A. Souther

Questions from the Universe:

- What has paralyzed you with fear?

- How do you regain faith in yourself?

- What do you need to become whole?

- How do you take that final leap of faith into the vast universe?

- What is the next step in the evolution of your soul?

The Heart Of Tarot

PROTECTION

SAFETY
GUARDIAN
SHIELD
DEFENSE
SHELTER

Protection represents the **safety** of an invisible yet strong circle drawn around the perimeters of Self. Imagine a **guardian** stepping in when there was a threat. Imagine the higher Self stands at careful attention, always watching, always ready to send an intuitive warning for the slightest danger.

There are times when the uncertainty of circumstances will make you feel threatened. Then, you can pull your energy **shield** up to create a circle or a magic bubble. You have the power to invoke protection at any given moment in time. But first, you have to know when your boundaries are in jeopardy.

You must listen to the inner voice that speaks when your foundations are shaking and your walls are ready to fall. You can often not protect yourself by shutting others out, yet it is necessary to provide defense for yourself. The exposure to external threats to your identity is your priority. You must **shelter** and safeguard yourself from harm on all four levels: heart, mind, body, and spirit.

Protection's shadow tends to create a place so heavily defended that no one can get in. It is possible to shut out human contact or, at the very least, filter most levels of communication through your armor. You find yourself only allowing things you agree with to sift through.

You must be aware to invoke your protective nature when necessary but not let the safeguards become a problem in communication. Your heart must be open. Your mind must be receptive. Your body must be trained. Your spirit must be creative. Otherwise, you will live a lonely existence, cut off from the joys of life.

Protection calls for solid boundaries. Find the place within that instinctively knows the danger and heed the voice. At the same time, listen to the heart when it asks for forgiveness and shared pleasure. Listen to the intellect as it advises. Listen to the body as it senses the physical surroundings. And finally, listen to the spirit, the higher Self, as intuition is the guiding force.

Questions from Protection:

- When has your guardian blocked all forms of communication?

- How have you kept yourself isolated with too much protection?

- How do you ensure you are protected and not vulnerable to harm?

- What brings balance between too much and not enough boundaries?

- How does your intuition support you?

The Heart Of Tarot

THE MINOR ARCANA

*the discovery
of how
Self survives in
the wilderness of life*

Dr. Ruth A. Souther

THE QUEST: FINDING BALANCE

The Minor Arcana (Ace – 10) represents the daily lessons, or the pitfalls, on the way to success. The four elements are represented within the suits: Fire (Wands), Air (Swords), Earth (Disks), and Water (Cups). With these mysteries firmly solved, you move toward the dream of a balanced and united existence.

Wands = *Lessons of the Spirit.*

> Ideas. New perceptions, personal integrity, authentic voice, or a place to hide. Seek that which lies within or never see that which is outward.

Swords = *Lessons of the Mind.*

> Communication. Words can be as sharp as a blade, cutting deeply, leaving wounds, or words can soothe the spirit and bring healing.

Disks = *Lessons of the Body.*

> Reality. Hard work, well-oiled machinery, in sync with the world, or ground to a halt through lack of care with wheels spinning in a rut.

Cups = *Lessons of the Heart.*

> Emotions. Flowing majestically, bringing growth to each flower, or all damned up, the roots tangled and mired in an emotional swamp.

SPIRIT IS THE VOICE OF AUTHENTICITY FORGED WITHIN THE FIRES OF TRUTH

Dr. Ruth A. Souther

The Wands

ACE of WANDS (Life Force)

    Ecstatic Possibilities, Passionate Action, Focused Intentions, Endless Possibilities, Independent Will Power

TWO of WANDS (Dominion)

    Energetic Balance, Genuine Integration, Inner Power, Valid Regeneration, Personal Authority

THREE of WANDS (Virtue)

    Personal Integrity, Moral Foresight, Dynamic Energy. Pristine Boldness, Radiant Creativity

FOUR of WANDS (Completion)

    Euphoric Achievement, Authentic Optimism, Crossroads of Change, New Direction, Self-Created Destiny

FIVE of WANDS (Strife)

    Energetic Conflict, Restrictive Patterns Inner Anxiety, Conquer Obstacles, Dominant Priorities

SIX of WANDS (Victory)

    Self-Confidence, Primal Expectations, External Success, Personal Triumph, Internal Intuition

SEVEN of WANDS (Valour)

    Personal Values, Intrinsic Courage, Accumulated Wisdom, Firm Convictions, Buoyant Regeneration

EIGHT of WANDS (Swiftness)

    Intuitive Communication, Active Vocalization, Internal Enthusiasm, Positive Reinforcement, Spiritual Fulfillment

NINE of WANDS (Strength)

    Spiritual Perseverance, Strength of Character, Concentrated Discipline, True Identity, Universal Lessons

TEN of WANDS (Oppression)

    Spiritual Repression, Resentful Atmosphere, Self-Imposed Injustice, Empowered Soul, Accept Responsibility

The Heart Of Tarot

ACE of WANDS
(Life Force)

ULTIMATE SPIRIT
ECSTATIC SPONTANEITY
PASSIONATE ACTION
FOCUSED ATTENTION
ENDLESS POSSIBILITIES

Astrological Note: None
Element: Fire

The Ace of Wands represents the **ultimate spirit**—the life force—that unseen yet highly felt **ecstatic spontaneity**. Reaching toward the impossible dream is an action that takes focus and determination. The energy of the Ace directs this stream of conscious force into accomplishments deriving from a place of integrity. The Ace of Wands doesn't have an astrological notation but is the ability to burn brightly with **passionate action** and **focused attention**.

The first step to higher consciousness is a desire for self-growth. With the Ace of Wands, there are **endless possibilities** to embrace your ideas, reach for inspiration in the most minor things, and motivate yourself to outstanding achievements.

The main ingredient for this spark to set fire to a multitude of options is the concentration of personal willpower. This attitude will never allow an obstacle to get in the way. Reaching beyond the limits of physical reality and into the stream of higher consciousness will bring great personal rewards.

The Ace of Wands' shadow tends to dissolve into impotence or the inability to see beyond what is right in front of you. The need for instant gratification can bring a sputtering halt to your creative process and the possibility of missing the most critical piece of the puzzle.

You could lose all momentum because you have not fulfilled these higher ambitions you set for yourself in your momentary enthusiasm. It is easier to dream than to act upon the higher principles of the Ace. It would be simple to accept the overwhelming sense that you cannot possibly live up to your declarations of intent, and ultimately, you will become unavailable and ineffectual.

The Ace of Wands expresses the sincere desire to achieve great things. Find the greatness within and move into action.

Dr. Ruth A. Souther

Questions from the Ace of Wands:

- What inspires you to do great things?

- How do you manifest that inspiration?

- What new opportunity is waiting for you?

- What motivates you to accept the opportunity?

- What has kept you from fulfilling your ambitions?

The Heart Of Tarot

TWO of WANDS
(Dominion)

**ENERGETIC BALANCE
GENUINE INTEGRATION
INNER POWER
VALID REGENERATION
PERSONAL AUTHORITY**

**Astrological Note: Mars in Aries
Element: Fire**

The Two of Wands represents **energetic balance**. To have **genuine integration** between the vision for the future and physical reality, the individual must first take stock of spiritual growth. The Two of Wands is the ability to gain dominion over ideas through external action.

Much of life cannot be controlled, but you can have confidence in your truth. You have spiritually awakened and sought knowledge to better yourself, which comes with the stability of **inner power**. You discover the way to **valid regeneration** is after experiencing loss and disappointment.

Notice the dualities in life and compare the values between what you have learned and what is taking place in the present. The mysteries begin to unlock as you look at life from an internal perspective. The process of moving that same perspective to external reality by integrating the known with present lessons brings legitimacy to your life.

The Two of Wands' shadow often makes your ideas twisted and dishonest. Remember, a sincere examination of your motives will serve you better than ignoring the truth. **Personal authority** permits you to act in your defense but does not allow for the abuse of power.

To have true dominion over your life, you may need to see yourself for who you truly are beyond the emotional mask, words, and physical manifestations. If you seek stability within yourself, the energetic balance point becomes a genuine appreciation for the gifts you offer to the world.

The Two of Wands offers the opportunity to find something great within and take the first step to an outward possibility. First, you must believe in yourself.

Questions from the Two of Wands:

- Where do you find balance in your life?

- How do you experience regeneration?

- What is the symbol of your authority?

- What motivates you to integrate new lessons into old standards?

- When have you been dishonest with yourself?

The Heart Of Tarot

THREE of WANDS
(Virtue)

PERSONAL INTEGRITY
MORAL FORESIGHT
DYNAMIC ENERGY
PRISTINE BOLDNESS
RADIANT CREATIVITY

Astrological Note: Sun in Aries
Element: Fire

The Three of Wands represents **personal integrity**, symbolizing the virtue of finding union within the heart, mind, and body. The Three of Wands is the ability to align emotion, thought, and physical action with spiritual truth for success.

When all phases of your being are conjoined to generate a whole experience, you operate from a place of true integrity and **moral foresight**. The face presented to the world is then one of **dynamic energy**, which, when carried forward, brings untold advantages. You create your prospects when you move forward with pristine boldness born of courage and independence.

With this idea sparking possibilities, there is no loss of identity when seeking your highest potential. When you present yourself from a place of honesty and learn to integrate all aspects of yourself, you allow your path to unfold naturally. Your future becomes bright, drawing you toward personal achievement.

The Three of Wands' shadow can become exhausted when putting up a front. Without the assimilation of body, mind, heart, and soul, there is no sense of bonding and personal strength. A large hole is created that siphons off your vitality, leaving you drained and weak. Your efforts are frustrated, and your dreams are derailed.

You might be inclined to place unrealistic expectations upon yourself, creating frustration and a splintering of character. Integrity fades as distrust builds, and your focus may become distorted. You then may be unable to function correctly, and your path diverts from actual achievement.

*The Three of Wands asks that **radiant creativity** be allowed to shine so others may see it. Be truthful within, and all that is authentic will flow outward. Find your inner light and let it out.*

Dr. Ruth A. Souther

Questions from the Three of Wands:

- What symbolizes your integrity?

- How do you integrate into one healthy personality?

- Where do your ambitions lie?

- What do you envision for your future?

- What are your unrealistic expectations?

The Heart Of Tarot

FOUR of WANDS
(Completion)

EUPHORIC ACHIEVEMENT
AUTHENTIC OPTIMISM
CROSSROADS OF CHANGE
NEW DIRECTION
SELF-CREATED DESTINY

Astrology Note: Venus in Aries
Element: Fire

The Four of Wands represents **euphoric achievement**. Once those chosen tasks are complete, a deep sense of pride and authentic optimism follows. The Four of Wands is the ability to celebrate the beauty of accomplishment.

The human psyche demands that you periodically take stock of where you are on your chosen path, and you often do that with a grand ceremony. The purpose is to acknowledge that you stand at the **crossroads of change** and, more importantly, are ready to change.

One intention has concluded; another purpose is just beginning. The fruits of your current labor will feed you as you go into your next life phase. By accepting this **new direction** as a **self-created destiny**, you begin to manifest your dreams.

The Four of Wands' shadow tends to linger too long in that accomplishment and forget you need to move forward. Resting on your laurels for a short time is all well and good, as you need to recognize your achievements and take time to realign your ambitions.

However, when you get caught up in the adoration of the moment, you may lose your sense of direction.

To remain true to your goals, you must strive to stay balanced and authentic with your thoughts, emotions, physical presence, and ideals. Finishing one project leads to the initiation of another.

The Four of Wands is the knowledge that completion carries the tide of creativity forward. Moving in the direction driven by intuition will serve as a signpost of good faith. Go forth and create.

Questions from Four of Wands:

- What have you completed in your life?

- What allows you to celebrate the changes?

- What new direction calls to you?

- What holds you back from self-recognition?

- How do you shake off apathy and get started on the next plan?

The Heart Of Tarot

FIVE of WANDS
(Strife)

ENERGETIC CONFLICT
RESTRICTIVE PATTERNS
INNER ANXIETY
CONQUER OBSTACLES
DOMINANT PRIORITIES

Astrology Note: Saturn in Leo
Element: Fire

The Five of Wands represents a state of **energetic conflict** that brings great strife to the spirit. Energy abounds, wild with the desire to create, and yet, the problem remains – what to do with all that boundless power? The Five of Wands is the ability to recognize the **restrictive patterns** that hold inspiration hostage.

Ideas are blocked by difficulties of your own making, which creates **inner anxiety** and frustration. You are not being heard, seen, felt, or otherwise acknowledged in the bigger world. You are limited and angered by these restrictions and do not recognize you have put them in your path as a self-destructive device.

In many ways, you are frightened by the prospect of such creativity. Therefore, you fashion situations with adversity to block you from going forward. If you fail to see old patterns holding you back, you may become bitter and begin the blame game. At which point you relinquish self-respect and responsibility for your actions.

The Five of Wands' light lifts the harsh boundaries you placed on yourself and **conquers obstacles**. Your energy will balance and allow you to initiate new projects. Recognize you come from a place of abundant power, and your light wants badly to shine in the world. Your fire is destined to burn brightly into the night sky.

You can abandon the limitations and race forward with your inspirations. End the stress and conflict holding you back. One way to achieve this goal is to look at your **dominant priorities**. Let go of those small things that no longer have meaning and the principles that once served but no longer reflect your truth.

The Five of Wands inspires the spirit by prevailing over the strife. Let go of the tyranny that creates a blockage. Go forward and embrace your talents. Shine your light into the darkness.

Questions from the Five of Wands:

- What obstacle keeps you from achieving recognition?

- What restrictions have you placed on yourself?

- What is your greatest priority?

- How do you achieve energetic balance?

- How do you embrace your talents?

The Heart Of Tarot

SIX of WANDS
(Victory)

SELF-CONFIDENCE
PRIMAL EXPECTATIONS
EXTERNAL SUCCESS
PERSONAL TRIUMPH
INTERNAL INTUITION

Astrology Note: Jupiter in Leo
Element: Fire

The Six of Wands represents **self-confidence** and the ultimate victory of fulfilling **primal expectations** on a spiritual level. The Six of Wands is the ability to find **external success** in expanded **personal triumph**.

As you listen to your **internal intuition** and allow yourself to be guided by your sense of what is true and right, you can acknowledge your experiences led you to accomplishment. Confidence comes only after learning to trust your instincts. You discover success is a product of believing in yourself.

To be whole and energetic on a spiritual level, you must be balanced with the physical, emotional, and mental aspects of who you are and what you hope to achieve in your life. You become enriched from a soul level if you strive for integrity around your victories. You can inspire and enlighten those around you from that place to reach their highest goals.

The Six of Wands' shadow tends to waiver in self-confidence. You may view your success with a jaded eye. Your perceived failures could outshine any triumphant moment. You could beat yourself up with questions that cause more harm than good. What if you did something different? What if you said this instead of that? What if you looked at it this way or maybe that way?

Hindsight will always tell a different story. If you do not learn to trust yourself, you will become so afraid of failure that you no longer try. You undermine yourself and no longer trust the intuition that demands to be heard.

The Six of Wands understands mistakes will always be made, but ultimately, the motivation behind the action counts. Be true to yourself, and victory will be yours. Go forward and claim your truth.

Questions from the Six of Wands:

- What represents the perceived failures in your life?

- How do your expectations affect your goals?

- What gives you a sense of trust in yourself?

- How do you manifest the self-confidence to achieve your goals?

- What pattern emerges as you examine your process?

The Heart Of Tarot

SEVEN of WANDS
(Valour)

PERSONAL VALUES
INTRINSIC COURAGE
ACCUMULATED WISDOM
FIRM CONVICTIONS
BUOYANT REGENERATION

Astrology Note: Mars in Leo
Element: Fire

The Seven of Wands represents **personal values**. It takes a great deal of bravery or **intrinsic courage** to trust in your natural abilities, creativity, and future visions. The Seven of Wands is the ability to find the spark of authenticity to birth that energy into the world.

The dreamer is often discarded as ridiculous, yet the world's dreamers bring significant innovations. Nothing becomes possible if you take too much time to listen to the voices criticizing your every attempt at something new. You must maintain your integrity and pay attention to your **accumulated wisdom**.

You cannot afford to lose faith in yourself, or you lose sight of your direction and retreat from your goals. If you bravely step forward with **firm convictions**, you experience **buoyant regeneration**.

The Seven of Wands' shadow dares to question along the road to achievement. Over the years, your experience allows change to happen. Your beliefs must develop. Your ideas must grow. Your goals must reflect your evolution, or you will become mired in bitterness, and the dark night of the soul will descend.

What once was inspiration has become a burden, and your honor will be lost. Look towards the higher Self to reunite with the brave warrior who will see you through the storm.

The Seven of Wands advises appreciating the opinions you offer to the world. Be the first to question the motives behind the ego. Success is yours when you see the entire picture.

Questions from the Seven of Wands:

- **What beliefs do you hold onto despite the doubt?**

- Do these beliefs still serve you today?

- What represents your values?

- What gives you the courage to present them to the world?

- How have you evolved through experience?

The Heart Of Tarot

EIGHT of WANDS
(Swiftness)

INTUITIVE COMMUNICATION
ACTIVE VOCALIZATION
INTERNAL ENTHUSIASM
POSITIVE REINFORCEMENT
SPIRITUAL FULFILLMENT

Astrology Note: Mercury in Sagittarius
Element: Fire

The Eight of Wands represents **intuitive communication** and a swift response to a moral dilemma. The Eight of Wands is the ability to weave the innate knowledge of the higher consciousness into communicating an idea to the greater world.

Individuality is often suppressed for fear of ridicule. You convince yourself that others will not accept your real identity. Your job is to weave the inherent truth of who you are into the ability to communicate your ideas to others. When you experience the rapid growth of inspiration, you must cultivate the outlet for **active vocalization** of your creativity.

Your **internal enthusiasm** is often ignored in favor of procrastination, which, in turn, defeats your purpose. It would be best if you found ways to organize your thoughts and allow the initiation of new projects to take place. Aligning yourself around your true character and acting swiftly upon your ideas will bring about **positive reinforcement**. This, in turn, brings personal growth and **spiritual fulfillment**.

The Eight of Wands' shadow mindlessly imposes your convictions on others in the mistaken belief your way is far better than anyone else's. Perhaps your way is perfect for you but does not serve another's purpose. And maybe you have outgrown your principles but stubbornly refuse to re-evaluate them because that would undermine who you believe you are.

The Eight of Wands offers the opportunity to recognize growth patterns as a spiritual being by communicating the changes that have occurred. Authenticity is claimed. Be yourself, whoever that is.

Questions from the Eight of Wands:

- What internal intuition is waiting to be heard?

- What action must you take to further personal growth?

- What belief no longer serves you?

- What pattern of growth is emerging?

- How have you imposed your convictions on others?

The Heart Of Tarot

NINE of WANDS
(Strength)

**SPIRITUAL PERSEVERANCE
STRENGTH OF CHARACTER
CONCENTRATED DISCIPLINE
TRUE IDENTITY
UNIVERSAL LESSONS**

**Astrology Note: Moon & Sun in Sagittarius
Element: Fire**

The Nine of Wands represents **spiritual perseverance.** The **strength of character** carries an individual through the battles threatening the greater purpose in life. The Nine of Wands is the ability to call upon internal integrity through **concentrated discipline**.

You have discovered that without honesty, your actions have no substance. You know you live in cycles and realize that not everything you ever believed carries over. It would be best to draw upon the wisdom of experience to recognize those patterns that no longer serve you. Nine is completion. Check-in to see where this progression has led you and what lessons have occurred.

To be independent and free-thinking, you must balance the conscious and unconscious and work toward strength on all four levels: mental, emotional, physical, and spiritual. Only then will you be able to complete your chosen tasks.

The Nine of Wands' shadow tends to get too wrapped up in a single purpose and refuses to be flexible. You may risk alienation from your **true identity**. You may suffer imbalance on all four levels, creating doubt and confusion. The biggest obstacle now in your path is you.

What is perceived as a strength of character becomes a burden and may cause you to become defensive. You stubbornly refuse to let go of what has now become a liability. Determining to succeed will be a positive factor if you maintain balance and respect for the **universal lessons** offered.

The Nine of Wands speaks to a narrowing of vision, resulting in a loss of original purpose. Know that cycles end and new beginnings are essential to the process. Stay the course, but learn to maneuver around obstacles effectively.

Dr. Ruth A. Souther

Questions from the Nine of Wands:

- What battle currently threatens your integrity?

- What cycle in your life is ready to end?

- How do you maintain balance on all four levels?

- How do you find your independence?

- What is the next phase of your identity?

The Heart Of Tarot

TEN of WANDS
(Oppression)

SPIRITUAL REPRESSION
RESENTFUL ATMOSPHERE
SELF-IMPOSED INJUSTICE
EMPOWERED SOUL
ACCEPT RESPONSIBILITY

Astrology Note: Saturn in Sagittarius
Element: Fire

The Ten of Wands represents **spiritual repression**. It manifests in physical oppression, killing dreams and creating a **resentful atmosphere**. The Ten of Wands is the ability to find a way past the restrictions of **self-imposed injustice** into new opportunities.

Because you can get trapped in old habits, there is a constant argument with your higher voice. You may constantly edit your inner dialog, which places creative blocks in the path to fulfillment. If nothing you do is right, how could you make a good choice for your future? The unconscious mantra "I am not worthy" repeats over and over until you believe it on all levels.

The heaviest burdens you carry are the bricks of self-oppression created by none other than you. It is a terrible injustice to your instinctual self if you do not trust your natural intuition. Your actions compromise authenticity. Your self-worth could be profoundly affected from the inside out if you are not truly genuine. You may find that every goal is in jeopardy.

The Ten of Wands' light side tends to release those old patterns. It is essential to realize it is never too late to recreate yourself. You are an evolving, **empowered soul** who aims to be whomever and whatever you want. The first step is removing the deception, camouflaging, and making a choice. Become visible.

Accept responsibility for your life and look yourself square in the eyes. Once you see yourself clearly, you may discover the past no longer has control. You can then refuse to live in the self-limiting environment that formerly suppressed your true character.

The Ten of Wands teaches that phases are meant to end. Move forward and be empowered to shape the future in a positive, healing atmosphere. Just do it

Questions from the Ten of Wands:

- What Influences do you resent?

- What phase should have ended long ago?

- How do you take responsibility for your future?

- What represents self-empowerment?

- How do you heal and move forward?

WORDS
ARE
THE VOICE
OF
REASON AND LOGIC
DRIVEN
BY
THE WINDS OF
CHANGE

Dr. Ruth A. Souther

THE SWORDS

ACE of SWORDS (Thought Process)

Mental Focus, Mind Expanding, Thought Patterns, Original Ambition, Severing Bonds

TWO of SWORDS (Peace)

Serene Mind, Opposing Thoughts, Balanced Resolution, Detached Presence, Mental Clarity

THREE of SWORDS (Sorrow)

Painful Miscommunication, Mental Reconciliation, Release Limitations, Negative Thoughts, Discover Forgiveness

FOUR of SWORDS (Truce)

Conflict Resolution, Internal Negotiation, Balanced Insight, Unnecessary Quarrels, Process of Elimination

FIVE of SWORDS (Defeat)

Irrational Thought, Logical Process, Impossible Standards. Severe Limitations, Examine Motivation

SIX of SWORDS (Science)

Rational Mind, Flexible Objectivity, Mentally Trapped, Reasonable Ideas, Intentional Direction

SEVEN OF SWORDS (Futility)

Mental Sabotage, Destructive Opinions, Helplessly Overwhelmed, Positive Planning, Rational Approach,

EIGHT OF SWORDS (Intellectual Confusion)

Deliberate Decisions, Blocked Creativity, Mental Obstructions, Ultimate Perception

NINE OF SWORDS (Cruelty)

Rationalized Criticism, Self-Inflicted Injustice, Devastating Doubt, Release Judgment, Honest Introspection

TEN OF SWORDS (Ruin)

Mental Paralysis, Hostile Environment, Defensive Techniques, Different Perspective, Positive Aspect

The Heart Of Tarot

ACE of SWORDS
(Thought Process)

MENTAL FOCUS
MIND-EXPANDING
THOUGHT PATTERNS
ORIGINAL AMBITION
SEVERING BONDS

Astrological Note: None
Element: Air

The Ace of Swords represents **mental focus**—the thought process—the **mind-expanding** ability to cut through old ideas and reach for new communication methods. The Ace of Swords has no astrological intention, but it is the ability to take the first step toward free thinking.

You discover a desire to expand your knowledge of your inner world and the world around you. In seeking ways to apply your willpower and forge new roads to travel, it is critical to understand that all things do not begin and end with yourself.

It is essential to realize you are part of larger **thought patterns**. You observe the difference between truth and falsehood, find **original ambition**, and work toward **severing bonds** that stand in your way.

The Ace of Swords' shadow is often unaware that failure or misuse of aggression and logic can lead to depression and lack of clear thinking. You may be unable to proceed with projects and dwell too long on unsolvable problems.

Accepting the loss of confidence and drawing back into a mental shell would be simple. These thoughts undermine your ability to fight for what you want. Learning to reach into your higher consciousness and divine support is critical.

The Ace of Swords expresses the sincere thought that each individual can reach beyond limitation and discover a new direction. Communicate clearly to find destiny. Step forward, pull the sword from the proverbial stone, and declare victory over old thought patterns.

Questions from the Ace of Swords:

- What new problems are you confronting?

- What decision do you need to face?

- How do you sever old bonds?

- What allows you to accept new opportunities?

- How do you view victory versus failure?

The Heart Of Tarot

TWO of SWORDS
(Peace)

SERENE MIND
OPPOSING THOUGHTS
BALANCED RESOLUTION
DETACHED PRESENCE
MENTAL CLARITY

Astrology Note: Moon in Libra
Element: Air

The Two of Swords represents a **serene mind** amid chaos. Inner quiet allows the opportunity to look at a given issue, situation, or relationship with clarity rather than confusion. The Two of Swords is the ability to take **opposing thoughts** and find a moment of balance and inner peace.

When a difficult choice must be made, and you are faced with no immediate course of action, the impact is felt on all levels: mental, emotional, spiritual, and physical. The desire to sit with your thoughts should be honored to find a **balanced resolution**.

To rush is to cause more uncertainty. Take time to meditate on the issues or circumstances from a **detached presence**. You can then grasp the answer that has been before you the entire time. Tranquility descends like a mantel of hope.

The Two of Swords' shadow understands these conflicting thoughts can fight between themselves and tear apart any sense of peace. You may hurt yourself with the sharp edges of your thoughts and create an unhealthy environment in which misunderstandings gain control.

You seek wisdom but may find turmoil if you do not take out each blade and examine the underlying message. Allow different perspectives to take shape, and through these diverse observations, you can sheath those damaging thoughts and continue with your current goals.

The Two of Swords finds mental clarity even in moments of indecision. Take a moment to breathe before committing. It is not always about choice. Finding peace within the chaos is reward enough.

Dr. Ruth A. Souther

Questions from the Two of Swords:

- What allows you peace of mind during conflict?

- What brings you mental balance?

- What issue in your life is waiting for resolution?

- What allows you to make clear decisions?

- What inner wisdom is ready to be of service?

The Heart Of Tarot

THREE of SWORDS
(Sorrow)

**PAINFUL MISCOMMUNICATION
MENTAL RECONCILIATION
RELEASE LIMITATIONS
NEGATIVE THOUGHTS
DISCOVER FORGIVENESS**

**Astrology Note: Saturn in Libra
Element: Air**

The Three of Swords represents an internal dialog of **painful miscommunication**. This is a place of deep regret, sorrow, things past that cannot be changed, and the need for **mental reconciliation**. The Three of Swords is the ability to seek forgiveness and find harmony to **release limitations**.

In the quiet space of introspection, you may find that **negative thoughts** override the desire for balance. You begin a review of your life, a litany of all that was wrong, which opens painful wounds with the sharp edge of your sword. You could alienate yourself from those around you and create disharmony by remaining in deep sorrow for what could have been.

You may fall into a crater of self-pity and become so deeply entrenched in separation that you cannot change for the better. Grudges aimed at ourselves and held against others do not serve the greater purpose of your life.

The Three of Swords' light heals the old wounds and lets go of the sorrow that has built up in your mind. You find phenomenal relief. You no longer need to make yourself bleed over past issues, but you can use your logical mind to resolve and release things that are detrimental to good health.

You are asked to relinquish the need to ascribe blame and release the mental wars that wear you down. Do not create hostility within yourself. Once these issues are viewed in the sun's bright light rather than the dark forest of insecurity and fear, they can be laid to rest.

*The Three of Swords is the signal to release old regrets and start along a path of healing. Connect mind and heart to **discover forgiveness**.*

Questions from the Three of Swords:

- **What negative thoughts impact your daily life?**

- **What old wounds keep you from your path?**

- **What do you need to know to go forward?**

- **How do you release pain and find healing?**

- **How do you find forgiveness?**

The Heart Of Tarot

FOUR of SWORDS
(Truce)

**CONFLICT RESOLUTION
INTERNAL NEGOTIATION
BALANCED INSIGHT
UNNECESSARY QUARRELS
PROCESS OF ELIMINATION**

**Astrology Note: Jupiter in Libra
Element: Air**

The Four of Swords represents **conflict resolution.** A sense of unity and peace is attained by declaring a truce with mental discord. The Four of Swords is the ability to expand thoughts into spiritual truth, thereby regaining control of physical reality.

This is a time of **internal negotiation**. What thoughts or ideas should you keep? What should you release? The Four of Swords reminds you that you can gain **balanced insight** into prioritizing the constant chatter heard in your mind with a new perspective on an old issue.

You can and should take one thing at a time, meditate on the importance, and then logically view the impact of that issue against the larger picture of your goals. The process is a four-fold experience that involves a review of emotional, physical, mental, and spiritual well-being and demands that you take time to find the truth behind the thought.

The Four of Swords shadow is challenged in resolving the mental bickering, which can lead to psychological shutdown and a return to rigid thinking. You may become mired in the current dilemma and be unable to find your way out.

Your mind could become filled with **unnecessary quarrels,** causing discord to reign supreme. You may find you cannot sleep, eat, or exercise and may become ill from the contradictions. Ultimately, you may sabotage your best efforts and fall prey to indecision.

*The Four of Swords is a message to quiet the mind and allow a resolution through a logical **process of elimination**. Have courage and discard useless thoughts. Find a place of solitude and meditate on the importance of peace.*

Dr. Ruth A. Souther

Questions from the Four of Swords:

- What conflict is uppermost in your mind?

- Where do you find a new perspective on an old issue?

- How do you eliminate negativity?

- Where do you need to focus your mental energies?

- What resolution is waiting to be discovered?

The Heart Of Tarot

FIVE of SWORDS
(Defeat)

**IRRATIONAL THOUGHT
LOGICAL PROCESS
IMPOSSIBLE STANDARDS
SEVERE LIMITATIONS
EXAMINE MOTIVATIONS**

**Astrology Note: Venus in Aquarius
Element: Air**

The Five of Swords represents the concession to **irrational thought**. Defeat is the acceptance of inadequacy and acceptance of false limitations. It is the inability to fight an emotional response with a **logical process**.

Your greatest fears are realized once you give in to negative thoughts. Integrating experience with new information is impossible as you concede the battle within yourself. Unable to find balance because of the chaotic views, you become a judge, jury, and executioner over your life. It is the Sacred Wound defining your identity.

You are convicting yourself of every conceivable offense and caving into the same **impossible standards** you can never reach. Once fear has taken hold of your mind, you can set yourself up for defeat. **Severe limitations** are set, which make it impossible to move forward. You may be locked into a regretful position, undermining your future endeavors and losing all hope of achievement.

The Five of Swords' light can bring these negative thoughts to the surface and **examine motivations** that propel you toward failure. This process will obtain the key to success. As you peel away the layers of negativity, you can heal the regrets, humiliations, and malicious and spiteful thoughts that seal you in a mental prison.

The door swings open, rational thoughts flood in, and you allow yourself to mourn those things of the past that no longer apply. You can then lift yourself beyond those old parameters and into a new appreciation of your ideas.

The Five of Swords is the opportunity to recognize limiting thought patterns restricting growth. Live life with healthy, positive thoughts to develop expansion into the future.

Questions from the Five of Swords:

- **What negative thought keeps you from moving forward?**

- What regret is uppermost in your mind?

- What allows you to release the sacred wounds of the past?

- How do you heal from these wounds?

- How do you move forward with positive thoughts?

The Heart Of Tarot

SIX of SWORDS
(Science)

RATIONAL MIND
FLEXIBLE OBJECTIVITY
MENTALLY TRAPPED
REASONABLE IDEAS
INTENTIONAL DIRECTION

Astrology Note: Mercury in Aquarius
Element: Air

The Six of Swords represents a **rational mind**. Problems are more likely to be resolved if the circumstances are viewed with clarity. The Six of Swords is the ability to find logic and reason during an emotional moment, which exposes the science behind the process.

The creative psyche often has many answers to a question, pointing to the heart of the matter. Usually, this creates confusion. To cut through the layers, you must look at each thought with a certain amount of **flexible objectivity**. Each idea deserves recognition, but ultimately, you must choose one to move forward.

You learn to recognize that two ideas can merge into one phenomenal breakthrough rather than splintering off to divide and conquer your energies. You truly stand at the crossroads of reason and must decide which way to go. There are times when inspiration has no explanation. You must follow the path that calls the loudest.

The Six of Swords' shadow ignores the obvious and fights against the direction you need to go. You can become **mentally trapped**. At this point, you often believe there is no way out. You may become inflexible, tentative, and perhaps even fearful of the future.

You would rather stand in the center of the crossroads, caught up in the confusion of your own making and refusing to take the next step. You could become your worst enemy by shooting down any idea that makes you uncomfortable. You must learn to present **reasonable ideas** to move forward.

*The Six of Swords is about accepting the unconscious thought process and allowing **intentional direction** to unfold. Focus the mind on the route at hand rather than resisting movement.*

Questions from the Six of Swords:

- What irrational thought interferes with your decisions?

- What allows you to be flexible when choices are offered?

- How do you focus your mind to attain your goals?

- What inspires you to choose a path to follow?

- What breakthrough is waiting to happen?

The Heart Of Tarot

SEVEN of SWORDS
(Futility)

MENTAL SABOTAGE
DESTRUCTIVE OPINIONS
HELPLESSLY OVERWHELMED
POSITIVE PLANNING
RATIONAL APPROACH

Astrology Note: Moon in Aquarius
Element: Air

The Seven of Swords represents **mental sabotage**. A sense of futility is cultivated by embracing the **destructive opinions** that surface during an internal dialog. The Seven of Swords is the ability to find every hidden excuse to derail potential growth and eliminate that negativity.

One primary idea stands out as the best course of action among the seven swords or thoughts. Instead of embracing a positive thought process, you may bring up all the reasons why it cannot be done. You might discover this is an ineffective argument, as nothing will be accomplished while you fight with your own ideas.

Your initiative is lost as you become **helplessly overwhelmed** with Too Much Information—most of it pointless and depressing. Rather than embrace the idea of **positive planning**, you could cave into the mental bickering. The more negativity, the more helpless you are to move forward. You may get stuck in one place.

The Seven of Swords' light tends to block out the voices that continuously undermine your ideas. Negative thoughts come from both the conscious and the unconscious. You can move forward by grasping the primary thought that supports your progress.

Becoming aware of the tendency is the first step. Catching yourself in the process of sabotage is the second step. The third step is dismissing harmful distractions rather than accepting disruption as a valid reference point.

*The Seven of Swords invites a direct and open communication channel. Talking out issues, expressing fears, and hearing the answers will shed new light on the subject and allow for a more **rational approach**.*

Questions from the Seven of Swords:

- How do you sabotage yourself?

- What are you avoiding?

- What is the uppermost thought in your mind?

- How do you dismiss the negativity?

- How do you take a rational approach to the future?

The Heart Of Tarot

EIGHT of SWORDS
(Interference)

INTELLECTUAL CONFUSION
DELIBERATE DECISIONS
BLOCKED CREATIVITY
MENTAL OBSTRUCTIONS
ULTIMATE PERCEPTION

Astrology Note: Jupiter in Gemini
Element: Air

The Eight of Swords represents **intellectual confusion**. Two ideas, two equally attractive options with mental arguments in favor of each, create enormous cognitive interference. The Eight of Swords is the ability to seek meaning within the questions and ultimately come to a decision.

You hold opposing thoughts in your mind, both firm and potentially correct, all with supporting data, yet you cannot choose. So many opinions are presented that you may become paranoid and fearful of the consequences of **deliberate decisions**.

You may not trust yourself to make the correct assessment, resulting in **blocked creativity**. You feel vulnerable and isolated, with nowhere to go with potential ideas. Your thoughts may be unclear, and communicating the confusion and doubt are impossible. You may be weighed down by these **mental obstructions** and become restricted in all aspects of your communication. Eventually, depression occurs when your emotions are tied directly to your thoughts.

The Eight of Swords' light resists over-analyzing every detail of the issue or idea. You discover the **ultimate perception** necessary to clear the debris blocking your path. If you allow time for the process, logical, rational thought will take over.

You may feel pressured by your need to control every conscious or unconscious situation. The more upset you are, the less likely you will find your way out of the mental fog. You may retreat and become immobilized. Instead, find your way out of the haze into the bright light of conscious decisions.

The Eight of Swords is the moment for bewildering thoughts to be sorted out. Let uncertainty fall away, and the path will become clearly marked.

Questions from the Eight of Swords:

- **What two thoughts do you hold in opposition?**

- **What blocks you from making a decision?**

- **How do you benefit if you choose one?**

- **What brings clarity to your thoughts?**

- **How are you best guided forward?**

The Heart Of Tarot

NINE of SWORDS
(Cruelty)

RATIONALIZED CRITICISM
SELF-INFLICTED INJUSTICE
DEVASTING DOUBT
RELEASE JUDGMENT
HONEST INTROSPECTION

Astrology Note: Mars in Gemini
Element: Air

The Nine of Swords represents **rationalized criticism**. Cruelty is the height of **self-inflicted injustice** when despair takes over, and all rational thought is lost. The Nine of Swords is the ability to reject guilt while aggressively seeking information concerning the source of serenity within.

"You are your own worst enemy." Absolute truth when you judge yourself as a failure. If you allow **devastating doubt** to undermine self-worth, you may wallow in despair because of perceived mistakes. You will be swallowed by guilt over action or, worse, inaction. Mental pain results. Shame and depression follow, as you know without a doubt that you are not worthy of anything good in your life.

You refuse to believe the decisions you make are reasonable. These decisions were valid based on what you knew at the time. You insist you should have known better or seen the situation coming. You could convince yourself that you avoided the problem or could have handled things better. You carry on until you are thoroughly punished, bruised, and bleeding over the tongue, lashing from your mind.

The Nine of Swords' light sees the repeating pattern of mental cruelty, and by finding the sympathy and understanding you deserve, you create an atmosphere of compassion and self-mercy.

If you force yourself to give up critical thoughts and take pride in the newly found ability to **release judgment**, you can heal the wounds of the past. You discover the drive and ambition to go forward through **honest introspection** and self-reflection.

The Nine of Swords begs forgiveness of past indiscretions. Let go of those painful moments from the past and present as they no longer serve the future. Complete the process and rejoice in your path forward.

Dr. Ruth A. Souther

Questions from the Nine of Swords:

- What perceived failure causes you pain?

- How do you recognize repeated patterns of mental cruelty?

- What allows you to release negativity?

- What brings you to a place of introspection?

- How do you find peace and self-forgiveness?

The Heart Of Tarot

TEN of SWORDS
(Ruin)

MENTAL PARALYSIS
HOSTILE ENVIRONMENT
DEFENSIVE TECHNIQUES
DIFFERENT PERSPECTIVE
POSITIVE ASPECTS

Astrological Note: Sun in Gemini
Element: Air

The Ten of Swords represents despairing **mental paralysis**. Negative thoughts ruin opportunity at every turn by creating a **hostile environment** that does not allow new ideas to develop. The Ten of Swords is the ability to overcome this opposition and redirect energy towards the positive.

You may second-guess every detail of a situation or relationship you are involved in. You may set up definite polarities or opposite camps of thought and build **defensive techniques** on each side to avoid a resolution to your problems. Worse, you could become self-righteous, confident this state of avoidance is the only way to deal with your concerns.

You might refuse to see that the cycle should have ended long before, and you are now the self-serving sacrifice. You will be exhausted with the effort to maintain your defenses and become hostage to your negative pattern of thoughts.

The Ten of Swords' light comes from a place of acceptance. The patterns of your life draw definite lines that connect the past, present, and future. If you can take a step to the side and view your ego from a **different perspective**, you see that everything is driven by fear of failure based on past events.

You base your decisions on what you know; if all you know is disappointment, you will recreate the pattern in an endless loop. This is an opportunity to start fresh by dismissing negativity and embracing the affirmative.

The Ten of Swords guides positive aspects in life, even during the worst trials and tribulations. Find the lesson in every heartbreak to evolve into a higher mentality.

Dr. Ruth A. Souther

Questions from the Ten of Swords:

- **What thought pattern holds you hostage?**

- **What negative cycle should have ended?**

- **What are the positive aspects of your thoughts?**

- **How do you become victorious?**

- **What has been the most significant lesson?**

EARTH IS THE GIFT OF ABUNDANCE BROUGHT FORTH BY DELIBERATE ACTION

Dr. Ruth A. Souther

THE DISKS

ACE of DISKS (Physical Presence)

Substantial Well-Being, Grounded Energy, Physical Limitations, Manifest Prosperity, Material Comforts

TWO of DISKS (Change)

Expanded Awareness, Positive Reinforcement, Tangible Manifestation, Opposing Dichotomies, Balanced Purpose

THREE of DISKS (Works)

Creative Diligence, Assertive Insistence, Self-Evaluation, Sturdy Foundation, External Distractions

FOUR of DISKS (Power)

Structured Values, Self-Responsibility, Lifelong Endeavors, Successful Perimeters, Impractical Spending

FIVE of DISKS (Worry)

Physical Anxiety, Paralyzed Productivity, Incapacitated Efficiency, Remain Grounded, Ample Opportunities

SIX of DISKS (Success)

Motivated Productivity, Effective Strategy, Logical Procedures, Progressive Experience, Physical Triumph

SEVEN of DISKS (Failure)

Fearful Exploitation, Physical Helplessness, Serious Consequences, Exercising Patience, Positive Reinforcement

EIGHT of DISKS (Prudence)

Persistent Self-Discipline, Cultivate Details, Different Perspectives, Experience Growth, Innate Wisdom

NINE of DISKS (Gain)

Successful Achievement, Measured Awareness, Remaining Balanced, Accumulated Knowledge, Maximum Maturity

TEN of DISKS (Wealth)

Enduring Abundance, Honorable Self-Worth, Good Judgment, Immense Ability, Universal Law

The Heart Of Tarot

ACE of DISKS
(Physical Presence)

SUBSTANTIAL WELL-BEING
GROUNDED ENERGY
PHYSICAL LIMITATIONS
MANIFEST PROSPERITY
MATERIAL COMFORTS

Astrological Note: None
Element: Earth

The Ace of Disks represents **substantial well-being**—the physical presence—the body in which spirit dwells on this earth. The Ace of Disks has no astrological intention, but it is the ability to take that first step along the path to **grounded energy**.

You discover a true sense of freedom when you accept your **physical limitations** with the understanding that these limitations do not dictate restricted boundaries in an emotional, mental, or spiritual attitude. You notice that strength and power are the rewards for hard work, regardless of the arena.

Embrace the newfound knowledge that your body cannot be separated from your spirit, and that spirit will take you wherever you want to go. The physical path begins with one foot in front of the other, and the fruits of your labor will **manifest prosperity** if you apply yourself to the work at hand.

The Ace of Disks' shadow supports your value on **material comforts**. There is a point where you could become greedy and suspicious of the opportunities placed in front of you.

If you choose to withhold yourself from interactions with others, you may remain unmoved and unforgiving and thus no longer able to relate to those who can assist you in your endeavors.

The Ace of Disks represents the ability to expand horizons to new heights while acknowledging the physical world's limitations. Evolve to achieve personal power.

Dr. Ruth A. Souther

Questions from the Ace of Disks:

- What value do you place on your accomplishments?

- What makes you feel secure and grounded?

- When do you isolate yourself?

- What new pathway is opening up to you?

- What motivates personal empowerment?

The Heart Of Tarot

TWO of DISKS
(Change)

EXPANDED AWARENESS
POSITIVE REINFORCEMENT
TANGIBLE MANIFESTATION
OPPOSING DICHOTOMIES
BALANCED PURPOSE

Astrology Note: Jupiter in Capricorn
Element: Earth

The Two of Disks represents **expanded awareness** in an ever-evolving physical presence. Change is constant and cyclical, requiring great vigilance to adapt. The Two of Disks is finding **positive reinforcement** while expanding to new horizons.

As your world opens up, the challenges become more significant, and you discover the need to acknowledge that change is a **tangible manifestation** in the physical world.

You must find ways to adjust and compensate for those ever-shifting boundaries and realize that the internal landscape transforms with the external. Your goal is to unify those **opposing dichotomies** and create a sense of **balanced purpose** that will take you further along life's path.

The Two of Disks' shadow tends to self-impose these personal boundaries and may become a wall that divides you from the reality of a given situation. There is a point when you could become isolated and may resist any changes.

You may turn away from the unfamiliar, refuse to allow the growth process, and further hinder your goals. Just like the serpent that must shed a layer of skin to survive, you must learn to recreate yourself over and over again.

The Two of Disks provides a lesson in self-awareness and regeneration, always moving forward along the destined path to the future. The beginning is the end, just as the end is a new beginning.

Questions from the Two of Disks:

- How do you see the patterns of self-imposed boundaries?

- What brings positive reinforcement?

- How do you create balance?

- What change is on the horizon?

- What motivates you to accept this change in your life?

The Heart Of Tarot

THREE of DISKS
(Works)

**CREATIVE DILIGENCE
ASSERTIVE INSISTENCE
SELF-EVALUATION
STURDY FOUNDATION
EXTERNAL DISTRACTIONS**

**Astrology Note: Mars in Capricorn
Element: Earth**

The Three of Disks represents **creative diligence** and the tenacity to accomplish anything a mind can imagine. The key to personal survival is the **assertive insistence** that life is worth every sacrifice. The Three of Disks is the ability to work hard to realize goals.

You can focus on the job and prioritize the developmental activities list. **Self-evaluation** is critical to building a **sturdy foundation** upon which your aspirations can grow. You see the power of getting a clear picture of what you want to accomplish and then heading straight toward that purpose.

Commitment to the task at hand gives a great sense of achievement. No detail is too small to address, and you discover you can break away from any confusion that stops you from obtaining success. You are also reminded that clearing away **external distractions** allows the body, mind, and heart to join. Once you become whole, personal power radiates from within.

The Three of Disks' shadow tends to leave the debris that surrounds you in place. If you do not work at clearing the mess, there is a possibility you may undermine your intentions. Instead of manifesting obtainable goals, you make mistakes and choose the more difficult path because you cannot see your way through the obstacles.

You may perform with mediocrity rather than excellence, which brings about your downfall. Boredom sets in, and you may no longer strive to achieve but become discouraged and unhappy. You may become too stubborn to let go of the goal that no longer serves you.

The Three of Disks is all about work ethics and a deep investment into future endeavors. Emotionally invest in the projects most important to self-growth.

Dr. Ruth A. Souther

Questions from the Three of Disks:

- What goal should be released?

- How do you find a new purpose to feed creativity?

- What gives you the ability to focus on the task at hand?

- What are you committed to?

- How do you express your power?

The Heart Of Tarot

FOUR of DISKS
(Power)

STRUCTURED VALUES
SELF-RESPONSIBILITY
LIFELONG ENDEAVORS
SUCCESSFUL PERIMETERS
IMPRACTICAL SPENDING

Astrology Note: Sun in Capricorn
Element: Earth

The Four of Disks represents **structured values** to build a stable future. Power presents its own set of rewards and risks, with the choice falling squarely upon the individual. The Four of Disks is the ability to have a strong sense of **self-responsibility**.

You must be practical and patient as you build the foundation to support your **lifelong endeavors**. You realize the necessity of knowing your limits and assessing your physical and financial boundaries.

To be balanced and secure in your decisions based on four-square reality, you must have emotional fluidity, spiritual energy, mental awareness, and physical well-being to establish **successful perimeters**. It would help to exercise your endurance to stay focused and alert to the possibilities presented and the choices offered to enhance your future.

The Four of Disks' shadow can become perverted by greed and the desire to control those surrounding you. You may find that power brings dissatisfaction and unhappiness. Your desire to accumulate possessions could produce **impractical spending**, resulting in financial disaster.

These self-imposed obstructions may limit your ability to move forward on your path. You may discover blurred boundaries cause your security to crumble right before your eyes. To avoid this, it is wise to stay balanced and question every impulse to physically and financially expend.

The Four of Disks denotes that the individual must support others to have genuine personal power. The fortress is within rather than built out of physical materials. Find the courage to unite the masses.

Dr. Ruth A. Souther

Questions from the Four of Disks:

- **What is the symbol of your power?**

- **What pattern results from your dissatisfaction?**

- **How do you protect your boundaries?**

- **What is your greatest strength?**

- **What keeps you balanced?**

The Heart Of Tarot

FIVE of DISKS
(Worry)

**PHYSICAL ANXIETY
PARALYZED PRODUCTIVITY
INCAPACITATED EFFICIENCY
REMAIN GROUNDED
AMPLE OPPORTUNITIES**

**Astrology Note: Mercury in Taurus
Element: Earth**

The Five of Disks represents **physical anxiety** and the tendency to become impaired by external concerns. Worry brings on patterns of preoccupation and uncertainty, which in turn creates **paralyzed productivity**. The Five of Disks is the ability to communicate concerns to others and to relieve undue pressure on the individual.

Your worries may become so monumental that they bring your health, finances, relationships, material possessions, and creativity to a grinding halt. You may create hardships through your uncertainty and begin to avoid the reality of your situation.

Hiding both physically and emotionally from issues becomes a real possibility. If you retreat to the safety of your cave and avoid interactions, you may create a huge energy block. Your **incapacitated efficiency** falls far short of expectations, invoking a vicious circle. Something has gone wrong, and fear keeps you from moving forward. The inability to move brings evasion, and evasion results in stalled energy.

The Five of Disks' shadow tends to **remain grounded**, both physically and spiritually. You will find **ample opportunities** to release the worries that bind you. You are blinded by uncertainty and feel a retreat is necessary, but you must guard yourself from becoming too isolated.

Worry takes energy and is exhausting. By staying consciously present, you can avoid your complicated past holding power over your decisions or demanding the future to fulfill your expectations.

The Five of Disks is an integration lesson to stay focused on the moment with an appreciation for experiences that create individual expression. Take one step at a time, one day at a time.

Dr. Ruth A. Souther

Questions from the Five of Disks:

- **What is creating anxiety in your life?**

- **How does this anxiety affect your productivity?**

- **How do you release the worries that hold you back?**

- **What reminds you to remain grounded in physical reality?**

- **How do you integrate life's lessons?**

The Heart Of Tarot

SIX of DISKS
(Success)

**MOTIVATED PRODUCTIVITY
EFFECTIVE STRATEGY
LOGICAL PROCEDURES
PROGRESSIVE EXPERIENCE
PHYSICAL TRIUMPH**

**Astrology Note: Moon in Taurus
Element: Earth**

The Six of Disks represents **motivated productivity** brought about by hard work. Success recognizes that accomplishments come together only after much individual discipline and focus has been exerted. The Six of Disks is the ability to reveal the dual desire for an **effective strategy** in both the personal and public arena.

You are motivated to succeed in your chosen field, and to obtain success, you must produce evidence of your work. You take pride in your achievements, and rightly so, but you must remember that you need **logical procedures** to be efficient.

To prosper, acquire the wisdom to share the wealth of your knowledge and motivation with others, generating fertile grounds for new ideas. Success begins within and radiates outward. Helping others achieve their goals brings self-respect and individual gratification. Your expansion is a **progressive experience** that produces self-motivated action.

The Six of Disks' shadow finds emotional satisfaction in your work, and remember that your authenticity plays a large part in manifesting your dreams. If you do not find the balance and harmony in that which you strive to become, the result may produce a large gap between desire and fulfillment.

Even with **physical triumph**, there can be loss and failure if there is no sense of sharing success with others. Success is fleeting. Always look for the next challenge.

The Six of Disks advises that to accomplish great things, first, examine the smallest details. Those details become the building blocks of the future. Growth is a continuous activity.

Questions for the Six of Disks:

- What do you want to accomplish in the future?

- What motivates you to succeed?

- What personal discipline keeps you on the path?

- What building blocks create opportunities?

- How do you balance this new level of productivity?

The Heart Of Tarot

SEVEN of DISKS
(Failure)

**FEARFUL EXPLOITATION
PHYSICAL HELPLESSNESS
SERIOUS CONSEQUENCES
EXERCISING PATIENCE
POSITIVE REINFORCEMENT**

**Astrology Note: Saturn in Taurus
Element: Earth**

The Seven of Disks represents **fearful exploitation,** which stalls individual development. Failure is a state of mind that results in **physical helplessness** to get past problems. The Seven of Disks is the ability to see the patterns that stop growth and thwart options.

Your fear of failure may cause **serious consequences** by detouring you from your goals. You may believe you are not good enough and have trouble finding confidence in your talents. The possibility of success may haunt you. There are always outside forces willing to undermine your strength, but when it comes from within, it is a crippling punishment.

It is indeed a dark place when you procrastinate and do not finish your projects because of these influences. You may become impatient with yourself and lose sight of the purpose. The desire for perfection is a cruel and twisting road. Nothing is gained, and brilliant ideas are lost.

The Seven of Disks' light observes the cycles, allowing you to catch yourself in procrastination. Examine the motivation behind the lack of activity, peel away the fears layer by layer, and discover the valid reason for this debilitating fear.

If you practice **exercising patience** with yourself and extend the same compassion you offer others back to yourself, you can dispel the fears that might otherwise rule your life. Step into a bright future by expelling the shadows.

*The Seven of Disks asks that fear be sacrificed in favor of the strength to move forward. **Positive reinforcement** relieves mental, heart, soul, and body stress.*

Dr. Ruth A. Souther

Questions from the Seven of Disks:

- **What is your greatest fear?**

- What obstacle do you place in your path?

- How do you dispel the anxiety that holds you hostage?

- Where do you find the strength to go forward?

- How do you find the patience to keep trying?

The Heart Of Tarot

EIGHT of DISKS
(Prudence)

PERSISTENT SELF-DISCIPLINE
CULTIVATE DETAILS
DIFFERENT PERSPECTIVE
EXPERIENCE GROWTH
INNATE WISDOM

Astrology Note: Sun in Virgo
Element: Earth

The Eight of Disks represents **persistent self-discipline** invested in the wisdom of experience. Prudence is the willingness to **cultivate details** that bring about the development of something rare and exciting. The Eight of Disks is the ability to view life from a **different perspective** while investing the time it takes to build a better future.

As you work toward your goals, you must be aware that perseverance pays off. A sapling does not grow into a mighty tree without the proper nutrients. It will not survive if the tree lacks any of these ingredients—clean water, bright sun, fertile soil, or a strong trunk —it will not survive. So it is with the human body.

You need the correct formula to **experience growth**, which comes with attention to the most minor elements. Show restraint when it comes to the physically demanding areas in your life. If you use your **innate wisdom**, you can overcome any obstacle in your path. To be prepared for the future, organize your skills and determine where the best use of your energy should be directed.

The Eight of Disks' shadow is subject to boredom by this slow pace. You may be tempted to throw caution to the wind and race forward, regardless of the sacrifice, to declare yourself the winner.

If you become reckless in your endeavors, you do not serve the greater good, and instead, you undermine your best attempts at accomplishing your goals. Maintain trust in your original plan so you do not succumb to self-indulgence and laziness.

The Eight of Disks advises restraint and the need to move forward with vigilance. See the beauty that lies within grow into full bloom. Do not undermine yourself with rash actions.

Dr. Ruth A. Souther

Questions from the Eight of Disks:

- **What small detail demands attention?**

- How do you prepare yourself for future endeavors?

- What tempts you to throw caution to the wind?

- How do you maintain trust in your plans?

- What beautiful idea is waiting to bloom?

The Heart Of Tarot

NINE of DISKS
(Gain)

**SUCCESSFUL ACHIEVEMENT
MEASURED AWARENESS
REMAINING BALANCED
ACCUMULATED KNOWLEDGE
MAXIMUM MATURITY**

**Astrology Note: Venus in Virgo
Element: Earth**

The Nine of Disks represents **successful achievement** as in the completion of goals set forth by choice. Gain is not about the triumphs of material wealth but is the gage of moral growth in the world. The Nine of Disks is the ability to find **measured awareness** while **remaining balanced** and in harmony with life.

Have you grown on all four mental, emotional, spiritual, and physical levels? Are you aware of the hard work and stability it takes to triumph over issues? Success does not mean you have gained great fortunes but have been fortunate to learn the lessons along the path.

Your accomplishments are measured against the strength of your character. If you can unify all that has heart and meaning with organization and wisdom, you become all you hoped to be. You reach maximum maturity by asserting your **accumulated knowledge** over the events that threaten to undermine the values you have gained over the years.

The Nine of Disks' shadow learns how to relax and benefit from the harvest you earned through your hard work. Destroying the ultimate rewards of your accomplishments to remain humble is unnecessary.

It would be best if you took time to enjoy pleasurable things in your life. Resist the temptation to belittle your achievements and take pride in your labors. The gains are easy to see once you have stepped into **maximum maturity**.

The Nine of Disks brings a sense of fulfillment and a well-learned lesson. Integrate the past with the present and look toward the future. Don't get stuck in old patterns that undermine the gains of hard work. Stay focused.

Questions from the Eight of Disks:

- What helps you succeed in times of stress?

- How do you maintain balance when events undermine your achievements?

- What allows you to integrate knowledge from the past?

- How do you determine the future?

- What symbolizes the strength of your character?

The Heart Of Tarot

TEN of DISKS
(Wealth)

**ENDURING ABUNDANCE
HONORABLE SELF-WORTH
GOOD JUDGMENT
IMMENSE ABILITY
UNIVERSAL LAW**

**Astrology Note: Mercury in Virgo
Element: Earth**

The Ten of Disks represents **enduring abundance** and the legacy that defines **honorable self-worth**. Wealth is not represented by monetary value but by the wisdom passed on to future generations. The Ten of Disks is the ability to express devotion to a higher consciousness rather than revel in the baseness of capital funds.

Affluence is often perceived as material objects, but it is not what you have but who you are that is of the utmost importance. Prosperity is when you acknowledge the **good judgment** you have accrued, the heritage endowed, and the traditions with which you honor a well-spent life.

Those spiritual, mental, and emotional values build the foundations that house your physical presence. If you look around, you can see the richness that belongs to you, from the tiniest treasure to the **immense ability** to recognize and receive the world's blessings.

The Ten of Disks' shadow understands, as incredible as this sounds, that a lesson in abundance is necessary. The cycle of good fortune comes and goes. Just as the wheel turns, what goes up must come down. It is also true that what goes down must come up.

You must recognize there is always a cycle to complete and another to begin. No matter how great life seems, this, too, shall pass. There will always be clouds to cover the sun, even for mere moments. You must maintain balance, keep the lines of communication open, and realize that splendor is a state of mind expressed in the physical body.

*The Ten of Disks takes nothing for granted. Every particle of life, both positive and negative, contributes to enduring wealth. Respect the **universal law** of order to prosper.*

Dr. Ruth A. Souther

Questions from the Ten of Disks:

- How do you define self-worth?

- What legacy do you give to the world?

- What do you take for granted?

- How do you maintain balance as life changes?

- What is the key to your prosperity?

EMOTIONAL HEALING IS FOUND ON THE OCEANIC TIDES OF UNCONDITIONAL LOVE

The Cups

ACE of CUPS (Emotional Health)

Devoted Receptivity, Compassionate Accessibility, Unconditional Love, Sincere Humbleness, Emotional Emptiness

TWO of CUPS (Love)

Inspired Balance, Healthy Affection, Hurtful Patterns, Respectful Relationships, Emotional Fulfillment

THREE of CUPS (Abundance)

Heartfelt Exchange, Happy Relationships, Solitary Existence, Lonely Burden, True Fulfillment

FOUR of CUPS (Luxury)

Indulgent Gratification, Internal Contentment, External Satisfaction, False Security, Material Things

FIVE of CUPS (Disappointment)

Unrealistic Expectation, Chronic Denial, Persistent Rejection, Transformative Agent, Emotional Healing

SIX of CUPS (Pleasure)

Determined Regeneration, Different Outcome, Conscious Awareness, Old Circumstances, Uplifting Path

SEVEN of CUPS (Debauch)

Addictive Indulgence, Excessive Behavior, Extravagant Patterns, Realistic Focus, Grounded Action

EIGHT of CUPS (Indolence)

Indifferent Exhaustion, Lethargic Discontent, Emotional Stagnation, Peaceful Awareness, Overwhelming Rejuvenation

NINE of CUPS (Happiness)

Abundant Expansion, Cheerful Existence, Decadent Intoxication, Restless Discontent, Evolving Development

TEN of CUPS (Satiety)

Complacent Satisfaction, Optimistic Contentment, Harmonious Union, Corrupt Intentions, Self-Indulgent Behavior

The Heart Of Tarot

ACE of CUPS
(Emotional Health)

**DEVOTED RECEPTIVITY
COMPASSIONATE ACCESSIBILITY
UNCONDITIONAL LOVE
SINCERE HUMBLENESS
EMOTIONAL EMPTINESS**

**Astrological Note: None
Element: Water**

The Ace of Cups represents **devoted receptivity**—the emotional health—that opens psychic, spiritual, and unconscious channels to **compassionate accessibility**. The Ace of Cups has no astrological notation, but it is the ability to take that first step along the path to **unconditional love**.

The desire to grow up and break out of old behavior patterns is the beginning of emotional maturity. It is where you dream of innovations and the ability to break into new ways of being. You have the grace to accept the blessings and gifts offered to you, however small or large.

You appreciate the beauty that surrounds you. Creating harmony within the chaos allows **sincere humbleness** to become a way of life. Through this open channel, heartfelt inspiration will enable you to embrace those you love and empathize with those you do not. Begin by forgiving yourself and healing those old emotional wounds that take control at every opportunity.

The Ace of Cups' shadow ignores the opportunities to heal the heart and rejects any kindness offered. A certain coldness may descend that could create an atmosphere of **emotional emptiness**.

The void within may grow beyond measure. It may become nearly impossible to extract any sympathy for your actions. The abyss is filled with deception, disturbing dreams, and feelings of powerlessness that may define the relationship with yourself and others.

The Ace of Cups is the process of true emotional health and happiness garnered by embracing the capacity to love with an open heart. Honor your feelings and extend your love.

Questions from the Ace of Cups:

- What emotional truth should be recognized?

- How do you define unconditional love?

- When have you felt emotionally empty?

- What new relationship is waiting for you?

- What motivates you to accept this relationship?

The Heart Of Tarot

TWO of CUPS
(Love)

INSPIRED BALANCE
HEALTHY AFFECTION
HURTFUL PATTERNS
RESPECTFUL RELATIONSHIPS
EMOTIONAL FULFILLMENT

Astrology Note: Venus in Cancer
Element: Water

The Two of Cups represents **inspired balance**. It occurs as the internal source of **healthy affection** flows outward toward the world. Love is freely given and just as equally received. The Two of Cups is the ability to open up to nurturing and fulfilling feelings.

Most importantly, you must learn to love yourself from a place of compassion and understanding. You are only human, and any errors in judgment must be forgiven. From this place of empathetic communication, you will discover an internal relationship free of **hurtful patterns**.

Without abandoning your values or diminishing your self-worth, you notice a deep connection with others, bringing joy into your life. Love allows you to be independent and authentic while acknowledging others and their values.

The Two of Cups' shadow tends to deny you love and blind yourself to your emotional growth. Then, you may become blocked from your creativity. Your inspiration springs from a healthy well of sentiment and a flowing stream of emotions. Keep the current clear of debris.

The duality of Love is not hate—it is indifference. When you can see clearly, you discover the greatest gift of all: self-love. Practicing equal and **respectful relationships** with yourself and others will lead to true **emotional fulfillment**.

The Two of Cups promotes harmony and balance within. Find a way to retain a reverent outlook on life and respect for all living things. Love yourself before offering love to someone else. Understanding individuals' processes for healing helps to smooth your way forward. Be compassionate.

Questions from the Two of Cups:

- When have you denied yourself love and forgiveness?

- What allows you to love and nurture yourself?

- How do you find emotional balance within yourself?

- What is the key to your creativity?

- What inspires you to listen to your heart?

The Heart Of Tarot

THREE of CUPS
(Abundance)

HEARTFELT EXCHANGE
HAPPY RELATIONSHIP
SOLITARY EXISTENCE
LONELY BURDEN
TRUE FULFILLMENT

Astrology Note: Mercury in Cancer
Element: Water

The Three of Cups represents a **heartfelt exchange**. Rejoicing in the profusion of love and the ability to share with others brings true abundance. The Three of Cups is the ability to hear the thread of sincere communication within the heart.

A smile reflects healthy affection for those in our lives, and laughter ignites elation and shared happiness. It would be best to remember that a sense of humor and the ability to laugh under challenging moments brings renewed self-awareness. Knowing your heart's desires is the key to a **happy relationship** with yourself and those around you.

Remember to celebrate your achievements with others and refrain from leading a **solitary existence**. It is that ordinary moment of joy when you fully realize what it means to bond with another. Those connections profoundly impact your survival in the greater world.

The Three of Cups' shadow turns away from sharing feelings, and you may be carrying a very private and **lonely burden** of exclusion. Events that should be filled with joy become meaningless and often reflect in the physical body as a heavy load.

This brings weariness and the inability to celebrate personal triumphs. You may create a sense of emptiness if you do not allow **true fulfillment** to overflow from your heart and give to others.

The Three of Cups describes a whole heart that finds great satisfaction in giving to others. Give without expectations and discover deep joy.

Questions from the Three of Cups:

- When have you felt lonely and insecure?

- What brings you joy?

- What do you need to celebrate?

- What feelings need to be shared with others?

- What is the key to your emotional self-awareness?

The Heart Of Tarot

FOUR of CUPS
(Luxury)

INDULGENT GRATIFICATION
INTERNAL CONTENTMENT
EXTERNAL SATISFACTION
FALSE SECURITY
MATERIAL THINGS

Astrology Note: Moon in Cancer
Element: Water

The Four of Cups represents **indulgent gratification**. The human heart constantly strives to balance **internal contentment** and **external satisfaction**, often creating a standard steeped in extravagance. True luxury is a commitment to emotional evolution and acceptance of the wealth gained from experience.

You try to convince yourself that you have accomplished your goals and that all levels of consciousness have been examined. The mind is secure, the body is healthy, the spirit is at peace, and the heart is overflowing with happiness. This **false security** you have embraced will most likely avoid the real issues deep within.

Look closer, and you will see you have built a prison made of **material things**. Wallowing in this artificial sense of luxury and avoiding true emotional fulfillment becomes a way of life. To achieve absolute joy, you should thoroughly examine the roots of this difficulty by untangling the illusive ideas that hurt. You can then begin filling your heart from the inside and allowing your contentment to flow outward toward others.

The Four of Cups' shadow often withdraws from relationships while seeking internal balance. Realizing you have been caught up in a false sense of satisfaction, you could refuse to take action upon new opportunities offered.

You could become passive and discontent during a good time in your life. Consider your options while fighting off feelings of foreboding that might cause you to retreat. Do not allow self-indulgence to circumvent your goals.

The Four of Cups brings the urge to daydream about the future. Be emotionally receptive to new ideas presented during times of meditation. It is time to create the foundations for the next project rather than contemplate what could be.

Dr. Ruth A. Souther

Questions from the Four of Cups:

- What is your primary indulgence?

- What goal do you need to re-evaluate?

- How do you open yourself to emotional truth?

- What brings balance between contentment and external satisfaction?

- What new foundation is ready to be built?

The Heart Of Tarot

FIVE of CUPS
(Disappointment)

**UNREALISTIC EXPECTATION
CHRONIC DENIAL
PERSISTENT REJECTION
TRANSFORMATIVE AGENT
EMOTIONAL HEALING**

**Astrology Note: Mars in Scorpio
Element: Water**

The Five of Cups represents **unrealistic expectations.** Disappointment results from **chronic denial**, leading to a state of vulnerability. The Five of Cups is the ability to delve into the behavior brought about by this state to begin purging unhealthy patterns.

You often cannot balance what you sought and what you received. Your heart often builds the perfect story: the mythic love affair, the bonded-for-life friendship, or the ideal career. And just as often, you are severely disappointed in the outcome. This position then makes you too fragile to overcome the disenchantment, which leads to a state of depression.

By **persistent rejection** of feelings that anything is wrong, you could end up in a glass house where everyone else sees the self-inflicted suffering, but you do not. You could wind up quarreling over every minor slight rather than rising above things that cannot hurt you if you do not let them.

The Five of Cups' shadow tends to acknowledge that disappointment causes an imbalance in your life. However, disappointment can become a **transformative agent**. Find the inner recesses of strength to push away the sadness and sense of abandonment.

There, you will discover the strength to change your perceptions. You must dive into the depths of your unhappiness to find answers. Once there, you can incorporate **emotional healing** into the process of self-discovery.

The Five of Cups is all about attention to the smallest details of disillusionment and the magic of transforming the negative into a positive step forward. Self-pity serves no one.

Dr. Ruth A. Souther

Questions from the Five of Cups:

- What is the major disappointment of your life?

- What unrealistic expectation drives your actions?

- How do you heal your wounded heart?

- What transforms your negative feelings?

- How do you take a positive step forward?

The Heart Of Tarot

SIX of CUPS
(Pleasure)

**DETERMINED REGENERATION
DIFFERENT OUTCOME
CONSCIOUS AWARENESS
OLD CIRCUMSTANCES
UPLIFTING PATH**

**Astrology Note: Sun in Scorpio
Element: Water**

The Six of Cups represents **determined regeneration**. Taking pleasure in even the slightest opportunity to grow in an optimistic and nurturing environment brings great contentment. The Six of Cups is the ability to achieve a positive state of emotional revitalization.

Although you view your past with a sense of yearning for what might have been, you must go forward with the determination you will not repeat the patterns that caused your distress. The problematic memories affecting your every step can now reflect a new slant.

View your experience as a personal evolution rather than a wrong direction. Take satisfaction in the fact that you are ready to try again, this time with a **different outcome**. Suddenly, the future looks brighter, your heart is lighter, and **conscious awareness** highlights the path to a higher understanding.

The Six of Cups' shadow is aware that memories from the past can create a deep sense of melancholy. Do not linger too long in the emotions surrounding **old circumstances**, or you may lose your progress. You may justify your feelings from the past and defend the resulting actions, which undermines the growth you achieved.

If you learned the preceding lessons, a sense of pleasure is earned. If not, you may become mired once again in the past and lose your direction. A heart that sheds unwanted feelings regenerates into a whole new being, the same and yet different.

*The Six of Cups advises that pleasure is fleeting and should be taken at every opportunity. Be aware of each crossroad presented and the future possibilities. Choose the **uplifting path**.*

Questions from the Six of Cups:

- What emotional crossroads are you facing?

- What allows you to take a new direction?

- What new opportunity gives you pleasure?

- How do you let go of old patterns?

- What no longer serves you?

The Heart Of Tarot

SEVEN of CUPS

(Debauch)

**ADDICTIVE INDULGENCE
EXCESSIVE BEHAVIOR
EXTRAVAGANT PATTERNS
REALISTIC FOCUS
GROUNDED ACTION**

**Astrology Note: Venus in Scorpio
Element: Water**

The Seven of Cups represents **addictive indulgence**. Debauch is a model of martyrdom that masks deep emotional pain and plays out in an unattractive manner. The Seven of Cups is the ability to recognize that harmony and balance were rejected in favor of **excessive behavior.**

There is a tendency to feel sorry for yourself and to wallow so thoroughly in your depressive martyrdom that you cannot see the harm these actions cause. Wantonly disregarding any opportunity to change your behavior may result in emotional muck.

It feels good to blame everything on someone else, which allows you to become the victim rather than assume responsibility for your feelings. This behavior may lead to fragile depression and send you deep into the fantasy you are blameless in the situation.

The Seven of Cups' light recognizes the **extravagant patterns** in your life, and you can correct your path. Beneath the emotional swamp is clarity of thought. When addictive behavior takes hold, you find yourself wallowing in your pain.

You must then reach past the sentiments around the situation and replace the emotions with **realistic focus** and **grounded action**. Thoughts and feelings are deeply intertwined. When one is grossly out of balance, look to the other to provide a counterweight.

The Seven of Cups brings forth the possibility of delusional and indulgent behavior and the desire to embrace the outcome rather than attempt to change it. Such an outlook stalls growth, which is no longer emotionally functional. Use compassion to heal destructive feelings.

Questions from the Seven of Cups:

- How do you emotionally indulge yourself?

- What is the key to changing addictive patterns?

- How do you find the balance between emotions and thoughts?

- What brings focus and a plan of action?

- How do you heal yourself?

The Heart Of Tarot

EIGHT of CUPS
(Indolence)

Indifferent Exhaustion
Lethargic Discontent
Emotional Stagnation
Peaceful Awareness
Overwhelming Rejuvenation

Astrology Note: Saturn in Pisces
Element: Water

The Eight of Cups represents **indifferent exhaustion**. Indolence is the act of passive aimlessness that leads to doubt and regret. The Eight of Cups is the ability to overcome intense and misleading emotional bankruptcy.

You cannot fulfill the emotional needs of others, let alone yourself. After giving and giving, you may be drained of the ability to feel love and joy. You may become so detached you refuse to accept any offer of sympathy or compassion. You may be locked into a pattern of **lethargic discontent** and find fault with everything, primarily with yourself.

At this point, you are convinced you do not deserve happiness, and the **emotional stagnation** takes over. Fatigue may deprive you of the ability to change the patterns in your life. Sailing aimlessly on the swamp's surface is better than diving deeper into the muck. There is a sense of abandonment, and yet, the hope someone will rescue you from this lonely place.

The Eight of Cups' light sees this burnout pattern, and if you pay special attention to the signs, you can avoid this detrimental behavior. When your emotions become depleted and you lose sight of any joy in your life, you also become physically, mentally, and spiritually exhausted.

It is crucial to set boundaries and allow yourself to say NO. You must take time and learn to enjoy life in small but emotionally sustaining ways—meditation, a short walk, journaling, reading, painting, or anything that gives a **peaceful awareness**. The result is an **overwhelming rejuvenation** of spirit.

The Eight of Cups cautions against the unfulfilling patterns of a lazy and overindulgent heart. Find joyful pursuits to steer clear of stagnant sentiments.

Questions from the Eight of Cups:

- **What emotional pattern is exhausting you?**

- How do you avoid the deep dive into emotional truth?

- How do you let go of the irrelevant details?

- How do you avoid falling into stagnation?

- What brings emotional rejuvenation?

The Heart Of Tarot

NINE of CUPS
(Happiness)

ABUNDANT EXPANSION
CHEERFUL EXISTENCE
DECADENT INTOXICATION
RESTLESS DISCONTENT
EVOLVING DEVELOPMENT

Astrology Note: Jupiter in Pisces
Element: Water

The Nine of Cups represents **abundant expansion**. Happiness is the art of acceptance and acknowledgment in the pride of self-achievement. It is no small feat to be ecstatic, even for a moment. The Nine of Cups is the ability to discover a contented and **cheerful existence**.

You worked hard to get where you are, but aspects of society define satisfaction as egotistical. Therefore, you may reject this moment as **decadent intoxication**. Instead, step outside yourself and relish the abundance and joy of this brief period.

You brought this pleasure to yourself, and you deserve to own it. You have been through emotional difficulties and sacrificed for the greater good, and now it is perfectly acceptable to exhibit a moment of complacency. You earned the right to be happy. Take full advantage of this transient bit of delight.

The Nine of Cups' shadow notices this reflection takes up too much time and energy, and you risk the excessive attachment to material worth. You discover you find emotional security in objects rather than relationships. Everything is lovely on the surface, but emptiness looms underneath.

Amid the shining moments of happiness, you may see yourself as shallow and vain and become filled with **restless discontent**. You have gone down a difficult road full of emotional potholes, and it is good to be proud that you made it through, but you cannot afford to stop there. Your **evolving development** depends on knowing when a cycle needs to be completed.

The Nine of Cups defines emotional maturity as acknowledging happiness and the necessity to proceed with growth. Savor the moments of joy and move on.

Questions from the Nine of Cups:

- What obsessive attachment blocks you?

- What brings you a sense of pride and gratification?

- How do you own the pleasure of this accomplishment?

- How do you complete the cycle of emotional growth?

- Where does the next emotional lesson begin?

The Heart Of Tarot

TEN of CUPS
(Satiety)

COMPLACENT SATISFACTION
OPTIMISTIC CONTENTMENT
HARMONIOUS UNION
CORRUPT INTENTIONS
SELF-INDULGENT BEHAVIOR

Astrology Note: Mars in Pisces
Element: Water

The Ten of Cups represents **complacent satisfaction** that overflows and radiates outward in all aspects of life. Satiety is the feeling of **optimistic contentment** that fills the emotional well with good vibes. The Ten of Cups is the ability to exercise authority over decisions that affect the passionate Self.

You work hard to achieve a **harmonious union** between your inward feelings and external actions. Once you have found this bliss, you are filled with a sense of joy that has no boundaries.

There is deep significance in being one with the universe, a compatible, hospitable expansion that leads you to believe that the goodness surrounding you will last forever. Confidence abounds as your energy and vitality take on the impossible dream, and you know with all your heart that you can achieve your goals.

The Ten of Cups' shadow can be overwhelming and scary, no matter how precious this moment feels. If you allow self-indulgent behavior to take over, too much of a good thing can corrupt intentions, even with the most selfless thoughts. You must remember the steps that brought you to this point of satisfaction and acknowledge that there will always be another staircase to climb.

Even this trophy will tarnish if you do not allow the cycle of emotional fulfillment and wholeness to complete. You must not become narcissistic and take life's riches for advantage or risk the disintegration of innovative and exciting ideas.

The Ten of Cups reflects the maturity to balance emotional satisfaction with achieving new goals. Being replete is one thing. Knowing that the current cycle must conclude before the next begins is another. Recognize the phase is over and follow through.

Questions from the Ten of Cups:

- What cycle is ending in your life?

- What impossible dream can become a reality?

- When does self-indulgence block your path?

- What symbolizes too much of a good thing?

- What is the next step in your emotional journey?

The Heart Of Tarot

THE ROYALTY

*the challenge to overcome
and transform
all that would
defeat the greater Self*

Dr. Ruth A. Souther

Mastering the Challenges

The Royalty represents the obstacles and opportunities along the way.

    Princess = Examine the possibilities.
                    Step forth in wonder.

    Prince = Avoid manipulation.
                    Stay true to yourself.

    Knight = Ready to do battle.
                    Sacrifice for the greater good.

    Queen = Authentic integrity.
                    Success equals Mastery.

With Intuition (Wands), Knowledge (Swords), Compassion (Cups), and Truth (Disks) as companions, you have the tools to confront every obstacle with courage.

The Heart Of Tarot

What is the Royalty Challenge?

The Royalty—or Court cards—and the mysteries behind their meanings are the core of Tarot. They represent the Archetypes that show you that change is imminent. You can approach the challenge or find yourself dragged, kicking, and screaming into a new paradigm. Either way, when the Royalty cards show up, a revolution is in progress.

The Royalty is the most challenging section of the Tarot to understand as their concepts carry the Minor Arcana Suit energies and hold the archetypical dynamics of the Major Arcana.

The Royalty is the challenge to step up your game. They are action cards. When they appear, they demand you recognize the moments that require you to fight for your goals.

The Royalty highlights the conflicts you face and points you toward achievement. They tell you all is possible if you embrace your natural ability, change your perspective, and take action.

Each suit describes the area in which the challenge appears:

- Wands = Authentic achievements
  WANDS ARE THE CHALLENGE TO BELIEVE IN YOURSELF

- Swords = Mental accomplishments
  SWORDS ARE THE CHALLENGE TO SPEAK YOUR TRUTH

- Disks = Physical engagements
  DISKS ARE THE CHALLENGE TO CONTROL YOUR OWN LIFE

- Cups = Emotional encounters
  CUPS ARE THE CHALLENGE TO LIVE YOUR INTEGRITY

Dr. Ruth A. Souther

VISIONARY ENERGY:

THE PRINCESS

The Heart Of Tarot

The Princess is unique as she dances to the beat of her drum. She is the Dreamer who sees the world around her through different eyes. Prophetic and potent, she questions structure and the status quo.

The Princess is the beginning, the creative venture going forth despite fear, who is willing to do whatever it takes to embrace the vision. She is the first step toward authentic fulfillment, mindful awareness, physical manifestation, and emotional maturity.

She is idealistic and believes breaking down any barrier that would prevent her from reaching her goal is necessary. She knows her gifts as she strikes out on her independent path. She is equally aware of her vulnerabilities and seeks to strengthen her resolve using all the elemental tools: Air, Fire, Earth, and Water.

The Princess is equivalent to the Page in the Rider Waite Smith deck, and although the Page is masculine and the Princess is feminine, they both hold the aspect of the curious rebel who questions the societal structure. They seek change, driven by an unquenchable desire to create something new from the old form.

Her energy connects to the season when all things begin to green, and the scent of growth is in the air. The Princess is the bud, just waiting for the right moment to burst forth in all her glory. Indeed, she heeds the call of the wild season and accepts the challenge to shift, change, and become everything she is supposed to be. She is illuminated below the conscious portal, driven by the purest elemental energy.

The Princess is Potential. She is the Spark, the Whisper, the Escape, the Flow. She is the Visionary by which all things are possible.

Archetypically speaking, she is the Herald who hears the call, the Rebel who responds, the Oracle who sees the future, and the Mystic who believes everything is possible.

The Princess—(Page or any other name—is the Royalty challenge to claim your visionary energy.

The Visionary Princess says, "What if my ideas disappoint, and I crash upon the shores of failure?"

Her Mother, the Queen, says, "Oh, but my Darling, what if you succeed? What if you fly?"

A Visionary has no limits.

Questions from the Visionary Princess:

- What potential are you afraid of?

- What spark is on the edge of your awareness?

- What belief holds you hostage?

- What future possibility is waiting to be unlocked?

- What defiance keeps you from achievement?

- How do you break free from false constructs?

- How can you put aside your fears and step forward?

- What does your inner Rebel want you to know?

- How do you shapeshift into the oracle?

- How do you become the Visionary for your life?

The Heart Of Tarot

PRINCESS of WANDS
(Courageous Transformation)

**LIBERATE SPIRIT
UNINHIBITED ENERGY
BOLD DECISIONS
TRUTHFUL REVIEW
ENLIGHTENED GROWTH**

**Astrology Note: Earth of Fire—Spark
Archetype: The Herald**

The Princess of Wands represents the challenge to overcome internal obstacles by being grounded in the present and allowing lessons from the past to affect the future positively. The Princess of Wands is the ability to project intuitive, courageous transformation into reality.

You can bravely face those doubts that hold you back and bring the hidden fears into conscious awareness. Becoming a **liberated spirit** takes work and dedication to avoid the patterns of the past. Embrace the spark of **uninhibited energy** that will allow you to make difficult yet **bold decisions**.

In the same spirit of adventure, you may achieve goals far above anything you have imagined for yourself. The blocks you experience could limit choices and the ability to move forward, but if you face old fears head-on, you can evolve into the next phase of your life. A **truthful review** of your motives will leave no doubt about the path you need to take.

The Princess of Wands' shadow sees the obstacles you seek to overcome can take on far more importance than they deserve. If these issues take on too much of your energy, the struggle to get back on track can be difficult.

You may refuse to let go of the old patterns, which can lead to the desire for instant gratification, indiscriminate behavior, and deep disappointment. If you allow yourself to embrace the obstacles, they can become the driving force in your life rather than something to conquer.

The Princess of Wands' challenge is to be the Herald who seeks an authentic path through the spark of integrity. Her pronouncement of authenticity precedes any proper action, as she must first find herself through genuine creativity. She speaks of imminent domain—the soul's true home where each prospect is carefully considered before becoming part of her reality.

She must first understand the underlying motives of her decisions. She must ensure they align with the integrity of her inner Universe before stepping out into the bigger world around her.

Why, then, is her first foray out filled with concern: Can she do this? What if she can't? What if she is wrong? Or right?

It is the crippling sense of fear that nearly stops her progress, but the fiery spark of yearning to be more—so much more—drives her forward. With one spark of her wand, the Princess lights up the altars that hold her hostage.

She wanders amid the fires, dragging all her dormant fears behind her, symbolized by a sleeping tiger. What is more frightening than a ferocious beast that could well consume her if it were to become aware of her vulnerability?

But the Princess of Wands recognizes the futility of hiding behind the doubts. As the altars burn brighter, she realizes self-doubt robs her of potential, and uncertainty prohibits her success.

She must face her worst fears and awaken the beast within, ask questions, shed light, and release the apprehensions that would steal her authenticity. She seizes the opportunity to weigh her decisions, own her choices, and step into the stream of consciousness that beckons to her.

She finds the courage to review her phobias and recognize those that hold her in bondage. With this release, she morphs into the acolyte, the student of her life. The Princess of Wands breaks free of self-made constraints and becomes the Herald of Truth.

Step into Visionary Fire Energy and become the Princess of Wands:

The Princess of Wands is the Fire Energy Visionary that reunites you with your purpose in life. She challenges you to own your worst fears, review your failures, and move forward, regardless of the outcome.

Imagine standing high on a mountain with the heat of the Sun on your head. You can see for miles and miles past the rubble of your life, past the roadblocks, mistakes, and fears that keep you from achieving your highest goals.

Accept the challenge to be authentic, to align yourself with a declaration of freedom. Step into the Visionary Fire Energy and become the Princess of Wands:

You pray for courage as you stand between unconscious desire's shadows and past actions' flames. You take a deep breath and draw upon your strength, deepening your Authentic Selves well and beginning to reshape your future.

You push forward with the awareness that you desire change. You want it. You need it. You must transform your life. With each conscious resolution, you face your fears and alter the course of your path.

You embrace the future, shadows, light, all of it. You are ready to burn the old ideology to the ground, to release the existing patterns. You see your doubts disappear into smoke as you recognize all the hidden agendas, beliefs, and history. You see the actual obstructions that block your way.

Do you go forward or retreat into the shadows, alone and fearful of the future? Do you extinguish the flames or light the sky with fireworks to celebrate your freedom?

Choose wisely, as the next step is critical. To advance, you must hold the torch of truth high and drag every unjust, fearful moment into the light.

You need only to burn away the crippling uncertainty to move forward in your journey. Easier said than done, too true, but if you do not try and retreat into the darkness out of panic, you may lose everything you have worked for.

You discover this is your growth cycle's beginning, not the end. It is the start of something new and ever brighter as it leads you into your power. The challenge is to fan the fires of individuality and accept your vision as the guiding light to the future. You become the spark that ignites the message of authenticity. You become the Herald of your own life.

The Princess of Wands is the opportunity to recognize and act upon inspired courage by exposing ideas that no longer serve a greater purpose. Take the first step toward <u>enlightened growth</u>.

Princess of Wands' Mantra:

"I use my light to face my greatest fears. I hold the torch of my internal fire to illuminate that which would destroy my path. I go forward with great courage."

Dr. Ruth A. Souther

Questions from the Princess of Wands:

- What truth brings your most significant challenge?

- How do you liberate your spirit?

- Where do you see the most profound personal growth?

- How do you achieve freedom from old patterns?

- What is your vision for the future?

- What propels you toward your authentic path?

- What declaration of independence is necessary?

- What is your unconscious desire?

- How do you maintain your conscious resolutions?

- Where do you find your guiding light to the future?

The Heart Of Tarot

PRINCESS of SWORDS
(Liberated Mind)

**VISIONARY IDEOLOGY
EXTERNAL ACHIEVEMENT
RATIONAL ANALYSIS
FEARLESS ACTIVITY
PRACTICAL ATTENTION**

**Astrology Note: Earth of Air—Whisper
Archetype: The Rebel**

The Princess of Swords represents the challenge of aligning **visionary ideology** with **external achievement**, creating a liberated mind. The Princess of Swords is the ability to bring forth a free-thinking, bold attitude that will change the world.

As you seek truth and justice through direct and **rational analysis** of ideas, you have the opportunity to advance your goals. It is necessary to break old patterns of defeating thoughts and behavior. You are ready to take risks once you can visualize your life without the bondage to preconceived notions about who or what you should be.

You can apply your creative ideas in tangible and productive ways representing your growth. Being a rebel is scary, and going against the tide is a fearless activity that requires much practical attention to the finer points of accomplishment. It is often painful to review mistakes or to see the old values that trap the imagination, but freedom is sweet and is achieved by hard, dedicated work.

The Princess of Swords' shadow believes the love of visionary principles will get you in trouble. Philosophies can become argumentative and overly defensive, and you may become paranoid and vulnerable when your authority is questioned. You can find yourself so immersed in the importance of your ideas that you fail to recognize your effect on others.

You may lose touch with reality through impulsive action and wind up wounded and surrounded by hurtful misunderstandings. You may be portrayed as the unruly rebel who strikes without a cause. Your actions may become meaningless and interrupt your evolution's liberated process.

The Princess of Swords' challenge is to be the Rebel who seeks conscious growth by aligning thought with direct action. She hears the whispers of ill-fated ideas and opinions, yet she continues with the Sword of Truth. She is determined to run a complete external evaluation of each situation as it comes up. She vows to assess her surroundings with logic and purpose.

How many of those views has she outgrown? She must consider each carefully and give her full attention to the altars she built around the philosophies of her youth. She intends to clear the path ahead.

She desires to break free from old patterns, smash icons of the past, release doubt and fear, and embrace the future. This task is difficult as it requires the Princess to look before she leaps.

Think before she speaks. Understand before she complies. It needs her to take authentic action once the desired course is set.

She stands upon the axis of change, one foot in the past and one foot in the future. She calls to her potential and the fathomless opportunities that belong to her, knowing it is futile if she does not first demolish the ideals that no longer serve her.

It takes great courage to release past expectations without a clear line of sight to imminent possibilities. Her actions are rebellious, even radical, so what is in store for her does not matter; only that she creates access to her most significant potential.

She is poised and ready to leap forward and embrace what will come. The mental blocks and internal chatter that littered her path are destroyed, crushed beyond recognition, and thrown aside as she makes way for success.

Step into Visionary Air Energy and become the Princess of Swords:

The Princess of Swords is the Air Energy Visionary that connects you to your fearless ambitions. She challenges you to own the self-fulfilling acts of futility, review your defeats, and move forward, regardless of the outcome.

Imagine yourself standing with a sword in hand, ready to smash the altars and ideals of your past. You race onward with a war cry, feeling the surge of righteous truth guiding you to your future.

You will not be stopped by limiting thoughts or barricades of the mind. You no longer pray to that which was, only that which shall be. As the Princess of Swords, you accept the challenge of being free and aligning yourself with liberated beliefs.

You stare upward in deep contemplation at the incredible blue sky, the bright sun, the puffy white clouds. It is a clear, sparkling Spring day, and you realize you have no limitations, including old concepts.

You spent weeks considering your path. It is visible and uncluttered. You believe your intentions are clear. A logical progression is laid out in a spiraling pattern right before your eyes.

Move. Walk. Go forward. Pay attention to details. Notice those areas of thought you tend to avoid. Notice when you prefer to gloss over memories or side-step issues. Notice when your beliefs become foggy, and you can no longer understand the meaning behind your words.

You've covered all the dissection, examination, planning, and groundwork to reach the realistic goals for your personal growth. How are your intentions impacted when thrust into the middle of opposition?

Expansion can be painful but also wondrous as you discover your true talents. Follow your truth and explore. Who knows what you will find?

The next step is critical. To advance, you must hold your Sword of Truth high and deflect every adverse action, thought, and word that attempts to defeat you.

You find yourself at a crossroads. There are many choices, many paths, all enticing, all frightening. You pause, realizing it is time to change. You desperately want to break free from those old ideas and eliminate anything no longer viable.

You discover the Rebel within has begun an irreversible process to peak mental capacity. False idols disappear, leaving the knowledge that nothing can stand in your way. You know the best action to take to achieve victory. Your choice is clear and feels right.

The challenge is listening to the inner voice of reason and striding forth confidently in your judgment. Do not hesitate to use your greatest weapon—your mind—to smash through the barriers.

The Princess of Swords offers the opportunity to recognize and act upon the inner revolt against a confined existence by smashing through the walls of inhibitive thought. Take action upon new ideas. Fight for the future.

Princess of Swords' Mantra:

"I can follow my path without animosity toward foreign thoughts and respect other ideas without losing my way. I go forward with confidence in my strength."

Dr. Ruth A. Souther

Questions from the Princess of Swords:

- What old pattern of behavior halts your liberation?

- How do you rebel against preconceived notions?

- Where do you find the strength to create a new future?

- How do you balance truth, justice, and your vision?

- What obstacle threatens your conscious growth?

- What external evaluation is necessary to go forward?

- What do you gain by releasing doubt?

- How are you empowered by liberating old beliefs?

- What is a practical and realistic goal for you to reach?

- What action is ready for birth?

The Heart Of Tarot

PRINCESS of DISKS
(Physical Boundaries)

**PIONEERING NATURE
PURPOSELY ALIGNED
ABUNDANT GROWTH
FIERCELY PROTECTIVE
QUIET AUTHORITY**

**Astrology Note: Earth of Earth—Escape
Archetype: The Guide**

The Princess of Disks represents the challenge to birth personal and creative power into existence by embracing physical, solid boundaries. The Princess of Disks is the ability to bring forth the **pioneering nature** of inspired vision by striking out on a new path.

You can produce infinite ideas and energy **purposely aligned** to achieve your goals if you recognize that strength comes from skills' silent, internal progression. Your determination to survive the physical hardships that block you from bringing forth your resourcefulness is in alliance with your need to be grounded in the moment.

Focus on what is necessary for **abundant growth** rather than setting your sights on what is further along the road. As you carefully hold the concepts within, allow them to grow at their speed—there is no need to rush the process. You may be **fiercely protective** of these new projects and discover a new determination to bring them to fruition despite the obstacles.

The Princess of Disks' shadow may take these ideas too far and experience extreme physical risks to advance your agenda and, sometimes, sacrifice everything within your reach to achieve this goal. This pattern is exhausting and unnecessary, bringing disillusionment and severe disappointment.

Often, you place the blame on others for your failed efforts. You may become angry and accuse others of getting in your way when you have blocked your talents. You can become neurotic and excessive in your behavior, alienating the power you seek to bring into existence.

The Princess of Disks' challenge is to be the Oracle who foresees the power shift and predicts the old structure that will fall. She quietly slips away, making her escape through difficult and dangerous obstacles. She knows survival hinges on grounded awareness as she seeks to release old habits and patterns that challenge her growth.

She has no choice but to flee the established foundation. Pregnant with ideas and a vision of a future that offers her freedom of choice and an unconventional approach to creativity is waiting for her.

She understands the old guard holds their course because of fear. They mean well yet cannot, or will not, alter their paths.

'Stay within the known perimeters,' she is told. 'You'll be safe there.'

But safety is not what she wants. The courage to take a stand bubbles up within her as she gathers the necessary energy to claim her truth. She is who she is and will not be denied her mistakes. Those missteps will lead her to her destiny.

She must go alone despite possible failure. And what is failure? It is a release, an occasion for celebration because she follows her rules, and it feels right and good. It is her choice.

She has learned that intentional labor brings excellent rewards, regardless of the outcome. The action opens the door to the next great idea, and she is ready to go forward.

Step into Visionary Earth Energy and become the Princess of Disks:

The Princess of Disks is the Visionary Earth Energy that empowers you to take action. She challenges you to defy self-imposed rules despite physical limitations and external distractions to experience significant personal growth.

Imagine yourself marching into a sovereign circle of potential, a clearing that appears as if by magic. You've walked a challenging path fraught with grievous perils and survived. You can now let down your guard and appreciate how your struggles have led you to a new life.

As the Princess of Disks, you accept the challenge to align yourself with a sustainable future.

The land is green and vibrant, blooming with ideas and inspiration. You feel the ground urging you to fulfill your potential design, the original plan born within you. It is there, right there. You can almost touch it.

The Heart Of Tarot

You sense it with your spirit, you know it with your mind, and now the job is to create it with your very being. Visualizing and extending your energy outward to manifest your dreams and tap into your originality is necessary.

With balance and fortitude, you discover ways to apply your aptitudes in tangible creations. Your pragmatic vision encourages the plan as you carefully cultivate your intentions.

To awaken your potential, you must root out and reject the obstacles and opinions that undermine your prospects. Set the standards you will continue to develop.

Your decision to escape the old rule brings great joy and a fierce triumph. However, now that you have expanded further into the physical realm, you realize others can see you just as you see them.

Standing proudly upon your abilities to demonstrate your distinct style, you acknowledge it is up to you to use all the natural resources offered to sustain your development.

You understand there will be trials, mistakes, bad decisions, and covert suggestions from those who think your mission is impossible. Your battle cry is "Bring it on!" for you are strong, capable, and creative, regardless of the obstacles.

As you draw your cloak close and prepare for the next leg of your journey, remember that every stumble leads you closer to emancipation, and every failure leads to your success.

Expectations create false security, so with great determination, you let the Universe know your desired outcome and concentrate solely on manifesting your dreams. Trust your instincts, for they are never wrong.

The challenge of sticking to your chosen path is not easy as it is littered with debris. Those obstacles seem impossible. However, where there is a will, there is a way. You will always find your way. Set your goals, remain determined, and overcome the complications that impede your route. It is your future, and it belongs to you.

The Princess of Disks offers the opportunity to recognize and act upon discovering remarkable things by seeking destiny with <u>quiet authority</u>. Embrace the inner awareness of creative power.

Princess of Disks' Mantra:

"I know the possibilities are endless, and I will create a masterpiece of success through hard work. I strike out on my own, certain of my future."

Dr. Ruth A. Souther

Questions from the Princess of Disks:

- What possibilities are waiting to be discovered?

- What hardships block you from abundant growth?

- How do you avoid exhaustion and disappointment?

- What are you willing to sacrifice to obtain your goals?

- How do you discover grounded awareness?

- What intentional labor opens new possibilities?

- How does this approach create a sustainable future?

- What tangible creations will come from your diligence?

- What natural resources are available to build this future?

- How do you hold yourself with quiet authority?

The Heart Of Tarot

PRINCESS of CUPS
(Intuitive Heart)

Emotionally Available
Honest Relationships
Objective Feelings
Remain Proactive
Self-Acceptance

Astrology Note: Earth of Water—Flow
Archetype: The Mystic

The Princess of Cups represents the challenge of being **emotionally available** and open to love. The Princess of Cups is the ability to be aware that an intuitive heart leads to **honest relationships**, both internally and externally.

You discover that you must love yourself before you can love anyone else. Now is the opportunity to state your emotional point of view with firm conviction and demand that you do not repeat old emotional patterns.

It is essential to regain **objective feelings** when plunged into crisis. Work hard to **remain proactive** and reject the reactive instincts that have caused insincerity in the past.

Suppose you acknowledge that you have worked very hard to move through the levels of jealousy, manipulation, seduction, or possessiveness. In that case, you will gain great insights into your emotional health, and **self-acceptance** will be easier.

The Princess of Cups' shadow finds the issues of jealousy and insecurity will lift their ugly heads if you give into your emotional void. You may find yourself resisting love, primarily love for yourself. You discover it can be too easy to fall into old patterns of low self-esteem, which leads to unhealthy relationships.

You may sway toward emotional dependency on others, suffer the loss of innocence and trust, and succumb to a callous, unfeeling state while ignoring your intuition. You may find yourself sinking into escapist behavior if not downright depression.

The Princess of Cups' challenge is to be the Mystic who seeks to immerse herself within the intuitive cycles of life through a deeper connection to her unconscious desires. She dives with intention and integrity below the surface, for her dreams can only exist if acknowledged.

Emotions can be dangerous. They contain all the beckoning moments of pride that lock her into the shallow end of her feelings. Sentiment holds the fears and self-doubt that can undermine the yearning heart. It shows elusive glimpses of what could be but has not yet developed.

She is cautious as she descends into her emotional truth. To embrace the struggle between immediate pleasure and true happiness, she must be open to the values of her true character. She must take a long and humble look at the moments when she allowed arrogance to supersede humility.

These are difficult lessons, but she reclaims her dignity as she immerses herself in the calm waters of self-respect. She sees the mystical nature of life as a current that must be followed to the end. She learns that she must follow her true calling, her heart's desire. Through that action, she becomes all that she is meant to be.

Step into Visionary Water Energy and become the Princess of Cups:

The Princess of Cups is the Visionary Water Energy that invokes your sense of emotional integrity. She challenges you to release chronic denial, old circumstances, and addictive behaviors and embrace the intuitive being that is whole and happy.

Imagine yourself immersed in a perfect pool of water with the delightful discovery you can breathe beneath the surface. Floating in the depths of your secret world, you can discern the difference between irrational response and balanced sensitivity. You choose when, where, and how to reveal your true nature. Until then, you remain a mystery to the world.

As the Princess of Cups, you accept the challenge of feeling and aligning yourself with emotional stability.

Your pulse beats with the tides, your body rolls with the waves, and you discover you are wholly and unconditionally supported by the heart of your Oceanic Mother. You come alive in water where you can honestly follow your organic cycle.

You are nurtured and cleansed within the sea-green depths. It is comfortable and comforting and becomes a place of healing that you never want to leave. Yet you know in your deepest heart that you cannot remain forever in seclusion, nursing past injuries.

You must shed the emotional burdens that restrict your development. You dare to confront the suffering that has limited your natural rhythm. You become bold, brave, and more objective as you look closer at the old, useless emotions that hamper your recovery.

Sorting the issues is therapeutic, and your awareness grows little by little as you discharge the wounds of past relationships and disappointments of the heart. Detached from the grief, you watch as each layer slips away, heading downstream to be healed.

Your resolve becomes firmer and more coherent with each pain that floats away. You can better hear the internal voice, allowing you to make better choices.

As your trust grows, your insights develop. You can consider the more significant issues and discover that flexibility brings more accessible solutions. You feel different. Sensitive yet protected. Your heart expands with understanding as unconditional love becomes apparent.

The moment finally arrives when you know without a doubt that unconditional love for yourself is essential to your well-being. Each moment comes and goes, never to return with the same intention. Each moment stands alone.

Open your heart and embrace the lessons as a learning curve. You will survive the pain. Become bendable and malleable, and you can incorporate all the sorrows that would otherwise deter your growth. Ultimately, strength and courage become companions on your journey.

The challenge is to trust your emotional intuition as you exist in the most passionate of hearts—your own. Vulnerability becomes a badge of honor as you strip all pretense and open to authentic expression from your heart.

Believe in the most beautiful dreams, be honest, deliver that heartfelt manifestation of inner beauty, and then fulfill your destiny by being true to yourself.

The Princess of Cups offers the challenge to recognize and act upon emotional security, allowing for successful and fulfilling relationships. Find love within before seeking love outside.

Princess of Cups Mantra:

"I balance the pain with growth and then evaluate my emotional progress. Rather than becoming a victim of circumstance, I become the victor in my life."

Questions from the Princess of Cups:

- How do you deal with issues of jealousy and insecurity?

- What allows you to remain emotionally secure?

- What symbolizes your willingness to enter a relationship?

- How do you maintain your objectivity?

- What can you learn from your intuitive cycles?

- How do you connect with your unconscious desires?

- What blocks your emotional stability?

- What brings you closer to your natural rhythm?

- What action does your internal voice advise?

- How do you find love within yourself?

DESIGNING ENERGY:

THE PRINCE

The Prince is the stable and cohesive designer behind the scenes when inspiration strikes. He is the Architect, daring and clever, he generates a plan to manifest the ideas, for without form, visionary concepts are just theories.

The Prince takes a chance at innovative and original thoughts by choosing deliberate action after deep contemplation. He is the second step toward true creativity, breaking free of mental traps, accepting personal merit, and understanding emotional perspective.

He is confident and believes he can conquer any project with due diligence. Hard work is the key to mastering a plan, and self-assurance grows with each opportunity. The Prince did not begin this confident in his own decisions. It was a lesson well learned after many disappointments and failures that taught moral values to an innocent. He never gives up, regardless of the outcome.

His energy connects to the season when life is in full bloom. When one flower folds, another appears. When one leaf drops, another takes its place. His productivity cannot be contained—the riotous growth as when the grass can't be tamed, and foliage is so thick it is impenetrable.

Within the depths of his wilderness, he is King. (Note: The Prince is pictured as the King in the Rider-Waite-Smith deck and other similar versions of the Tarot. He becomes the highest masculine energy in any other deck except the Toth.)

He is systematic in his approach, though it appears to be chaos. He holds the elemental tools that allow him to burn away creative liabilities, cut through miscommunications, forge across obstacles, and rise above emotional quagmires.

The Prince is Power. He is the Flame, the Call, the Drive, and the Wave. He is the Architect by which all chaos is converted to order. His action is to seize the day and transform ideas from passive inaction to unmistakable reality.

Archetypically speaking, he is the Courier who delivers the message, the Insurgent who fights for justice, the Sage who expands the experience, and the Mentor who sustains the process.

The Prince—or the King—is the challenge of owning your life's desires.

The Designing Prince says, "What if my ideas disappoint, and I crash upon the shores of failure?"

His Mother, the Queen, says, "Oh, but my Darling, what if you succeed? What if you design the future?"

An Architect has no boundaries.

Questions from the Prince:

- What is your biggest regret?

- When have you denied your ingenuity?

- When have you collapsed under the stress?

- What brainchild of yours was never born?

- Are you willing to expand into a new plan?

- How do you turn chaos into a viable strategy?

- What message do you need to hear?

- How do you gain complete confidence in your skills?

- What is your true power?

- How do you become the Architect of your life?

Dr. Ruth A. Souther

PRINCE OF WANDS
(Inspired Transformation)

PASSIONATE DESIRE
SENTIMENTAL DEPTH
HIGHER CONSCIOUSNESS
MAGNIFIED SENSIBILITIES
AUTHENTIC INGENUITY

Astrology Note: Water of Fire —Flame
Archetype: The Courier

The Prince of Wands represents the challenge to delve into the mystery of emotional insights with the hope that the artistic process can evolve to a higher level. The Prince of Wands is the ability to achieve a state of inspired transformation from a unique viewpoint.

The well of revelations is filled with **passionate desire** and **sentimental depth**. These two viewpoints come together in trust and spontaneity, during which you become committed to growing, expanding, and ultimately transforming yourself into a powerful expression of authenticity.

You must trust your instincts and acknowledge your inspirations come from a **higher consciousness**. Tune into these **magnified sensibilities** to have greater respect for your abilities.

You may discover unexpected talents that will propel you in a new direction. To be authentic, you must be confident to express deep feelings and not restrict or restrain the flow because of limited faith in your abilities.
The Prince of Wands shadow knows the intense desires that drive you to create out of your emotions may backfire. You can quickly develop a self-absorbed ego rather than become a self-confident artist.

At this point, your needs may supersede all things that could drive others away. You could become so tuned to your opinions that your ambitions will be frustrated rather than served. Your personal growth can become stunted, which may lead to anger and burnout. Nothing is accomplished, and the added layer of disappointment brings feelings of defeat.

The Prince of Wands' challenge is to be the Courier who carries the message of the Heralding Princess further into the land. He shouts from the rooftops that the

King is dead. Long live the King.

The old order has fallen as the massive, internal **yearning for change** takes hold and transforms fear into inspired action.

He becomes the leaping flame and the torch held high, the initiating agent with the key to the original concept born of the Visionary. He turns fear into a plan of action.

No longer is he held hostage by anxiety. He faces the light with his eyes wide open, all the better to see where he has been and where he is going. The shadows no longer hide doubt and worry as they are exposed to the propaganda that they are: inventions of his ego.

He welcomes failure as it signals his attempt to break free from chaos, that which would defeat him by stamping out his fiery nature. Rather than succumbing to inertia, the Prince seeks opportunities to advance his creative mastery.

The Prince understands the concept of expansion beyond a dream. He drafts the blueprints and studies them with a critical eye for detail.

What is missing? He pauses for a moment of quiet contemplation. It is then he realizes skill is not enough. Ideas are not enough; even the desire to succeed and actively seek his dream is not enough if the magic is not generated from the deepest part of his soul.

Magic springs from the depths of spirit. From this place, he can create anything.

Step into Designing Fire Energy and become the Prince of Wands:

The Prince of Wands is the Architect who guides your hand with fresh inspiration. He is the Designing Fire Energy that challenges you to develop your unique style and character rather than follow along with the crowd.

Imagine yourself in a chariot made of fire and pulled by a great beast that, at the merest suggestion, does your bidding. You are so connected to this creature—your intuitive nature—that all great things are possible. You place your implicit trust in the process that guarantees success.

As the Prince of Wands, you accept the challenge to BE original, to align yourself with internal illumination.

You've been locked into a routine of lethargy, stuck in the up-and-down energy of a cycle you didn't anticipate. A sense of restlessness within your soul has you longing for something besides the everyday grind.

You want to change. Change is good but frightening. Expansion, awareness, stepping outside your comfort zone to embrace different possibilities that are on the horizon.

Becoming the architect of your life is challenging as there is nowhere to direct the useless and harmful energy brought on by other's opinions. You need help, but you are alone. There is no one to supply the answers or who can dispel your fears.

You must face those demons by yourself and discover you have the strength to survive. You can pass through the regenerative fire of transformation and emerge on the other side unscathed, but only if you place your complete trust in your intuition.

The reins to your instinctive self are within easy reach; you only have to find them. The knowledge is there, but in broad daylight, you discover there is no need to grasp for control, flounder about, or panic in that moment of truth.

You need only to believe in yourself. Authentic, genuine faith. Not lip service, not false identities, but the trust that the fire of your bright spirit will point to your future path. It is a time of inspiration, enthusiasm, and desire. It is a chance to see that life offers many opportunities.

When you uncover your actual values, you can embrace your new-found authenticity with a renewal of spirit. From this place of self-validation, you embrace your path.

You are strong and capable, creating a holistic mechanism for survival. It is all or nothing—embrace the shadows, for the shadow is power.

The Prince of Wands offers the opportunity to recognize and act upon the artistic process by cultivating bursts of authentic ingenuity that can be fully embraced. Endorse and encourage creativity; feed the flame.

Prince of Wands' Mantra:

"I use this moment to find my authentic strength and sacrifice my fears for the greater good. I go forward with a renewed sense of worth and courage."

The Heart Of Tarot

Questions from the Prince of Wands:

- What allows you to recognize your creativity?

- How do you act upon your ideas without ego?

- Where do you find the strength to be self-confident?

- How do you bring emotional truth and authentic inspiration together?

- What change does your soul yearn to make?

- What internal illumination gives you the strength to trust yourself?

- How do you regenerate your soul's fire after a defeat?

- What shadow part of yourself leads to quiet contemplation?

- How do you immerse yourself in a renewal of spirit?

- How do you accept your true value in the world?

Dr. Ruth A. Souther

PRINCE OF SWORDS
(Inspired Mind)

INDEPENDENT ARCHITECT
MENTAL AMUSEMENT
BEHAVIOR PATTERNS
ACTIVE EXPRESSION
MOTIVATED DESIGNER

Astrology Note: Water of Air—Command
Archetype: The Insurgent

The Prince of Swords represents the challenge of releasing emotionally restricting thoughts and cutting loose connections that no longer serve. The Prince of Swords is the ability to join the inspired mind of an **independent architect** with a keen sense of self-awareness.

Inspirations are often sudden, intuitive, and brought on by unrestricted **mental amusement**. You reject the idea of blatant manipulation by your conscious mind and refuse to stay in bondage to your thought processes.

You may be bound to specific ideas and **behavior patterns** because of existing beliefs. You may be psychologically invested in those attitudes, even when the reasons are blurred. By accepting that those ideas are outdated, you allow yourself to break free from self-imposed restrictions.

You can then trust that your thoughts are **active expressions** of your inner truth. You become the **motivated designer** of your future.

The Prince of Swords' shadow understands the conscious mind may deceive the intuitive, emotional self into believing the restrictions are in place for your good.

There comes a point when you cannot trust yourself to know what you want unless you delve deeper into the intellect. You may discover it is better to be safe than sorry and accept the way things are than to cut free from exploitation.

You may fall into defeatist thought patterns, however destructive, because you know what to expect. The oppression is by your hand; you have placed the constraints on your imagination, and it is up to you to release the damaging control.

The Prince of Swords' challenge is to be the Insurgent who continues the battle begun by the Rebellious Princess to release old ideology and create a plan of action to sustain the new order. He calls to his higher conscience to assist, knowing that mental evaluation does not come quickly, especially when dealing with patterns of the past.

He becomes the Commander, the anticipating energy of the Visionary. He realizes he is in bondage to a blueprint established long ago that does not align with his current goals. He lives in an outdated model that serves no purpose but to create guilt, shame, fear, and stagnation.

Mindless chatter ingrained in his thoughts is the thread of deception that defies his aspirations. He can hear discouraging words from external sources that seek to undermine his attention.

These voices attempt to block his progress by throwing self-doubt and destructive opinions in his path to create a barrier he cannot overcome.

With a bit of shock, he recognizes these limiting judgments are aspects of his controlling mind. He stands in his way with self-defeating beliefs held up as proof that the only path is inevitable failure. If he accepts this process as truth, he will undoubtedly be defeated.

But he does not, for he is a revolutionary thinker who chooses to lead the mutiny toward self-discovery. His sword is the key to the original design, and he is not afraid to wield this weapon of liberty.

Step into Developing Air Energy and become the Prince of Swords:

The Prince of Swords is the Architect who gives you the strength to defy past failures. He is the Designing Air Energy that challenges you to purge self-destructive dialogue and redraw your line of defense.

Imagine yourself with your Sword of Truth held high above your head, ready to slash through the malevolent cords holding you hostage to your past. You sever those ropes with one mighty blade sweep and release all the negative energy. Inhaling a deep breath, you revel in the freedom and give thanks to the brilliance of your mind as you forge a new path.

As the Prince of Swords, you accept the challenge to be FREE, to align yourself with revolutionary thought.

You are destined to become something extraordinary. To find your way, you must mentally review who you have become and what ideologies are still vital.

Sorting is a brutal process that takes you beyond the superficial thoughts of success. You are required to dig deeply into habits and old routines.

You find that the words falling from your lips are inaccurate and dishonest—they no longer reflect the person you have become. You discover that you must balance past needs with future desires and authentically express yourself.

Once your thoughts have aligned with your integrity, you can do an inner evaluation of the present. Who are you? Who have you become? Do you allow reasonable doubt to become part of your thought patterns, or will you close your mind to the changes that have occurred?

To initiate growth, you must release long-standing patterns of thought. The old stories chaining you to your misspent youth have no bearing on your current path other than to serve as a point of reference for clarity. Notice how your moral codes have shifted and become sharper in focus and alignment with your goals.

This is a time of action, cultivating new thoughts and ideas and severing the bonds to doctrines that no longer serve you. Once these ineffective and weak principles have dissolved, you become whole, engaged, and ready to step into the power of your mind.

By embracing the emerging identity, you step into a robust future. You are reminded that you are the original pattern. You hold the pen that defines the details of the story. You can be anything you want.

The Prince of Swords offers the opportunity to recognize and act upon a deep trust in the higher consciousness. Do not accept failure because it is easier. Reach for success through change, however complex.

Prince of Swords' Mantra:

"I will remove the dogma that restrains my evolution and keeps me from growing. I move forward into a new identity."

The Heart Of Tarot

Questions from the Prince of Swords:

- What are your patterns of manipulation?

- How do you break free from restrictive thoughts?

- Where do you find the inspiration to express yourself?

- How do you achieve trust and self-reliance?

- How do you release the old ideology that has defined your past?

- What energy helps you with a complete mental evaluation?

- How do you disengage from the outdated model of non-productivity?

- What serves as reasonable doubt?

- What symbolizes the revolutionary thought to project you forward?

- How do you maintain a positive mental attitude?

Dr. Ruth A. Souther

PRINCE OF DISKS
(Reliable Boundaries)

PHYSICAL STABILITY
BASIC PRINCIPLES
MEDITATIVE REPOSE
GROWTH CYCLE
EMBRACE SUCCESS

Astrology Note: Water of Earth—Ambition
Archetype: The Mentor

The Prince of Disks represents the challenge to manifest reliable boundaries while building new foundations. The Prince of Disks has the ability to provide emotional support and **physical stability** during the construction of **basic principles**.

Your strength and sense of purpose are undeniable as you patrol your domain with a sense of commitment and security. Never rush to complete your goals. Take ample time to examine and choose your materials with care.

However long it takes to finish, remain grounded with a consistent interest in the process and with the knowledge your projects will succeed. You can sit quietly in **meditative repose** yet remain engaged in your surroundings while waiting for the **growth cycle** to complete.

You realize structure is of the utmost importance, for if the foundation of your building is not sound, the new construction will collapse. You must be patient and willing to exercise significant control to reach your goals. Allow yourself to embrace success physically.

The Prince of Disks' shadow understands your commitment to your goals will result in such stubborn behavior that you will isolate yourself from your community. You may instinctually put on blinders to avoid distraction, but this brings unnecessary seclusion.

You may attach too much worth to your ideas and become materialistic and possessive by rejecting valuable resources and suggestions to strengthen your foundations. You may become more engaged in the physical aspect of your goals and abandon the sentimental element that feeds your soul.

The Prince of Disks' challenge is to be the Mentor who continues the psychic

predictions of the Heralding Princess. He manifests the designing energy of a changing world and inspires a solid foundation to build upon.
He draws out the plans, taking a physical inventory of everything necessary to create the blueprint to support essential growth.

He is confident of his success and willing to expose his vulnerability to the world to accomplish his highest goals. He realizes all beginnings are helpful, though many are discarded.

False starts and bankrupt ideas are the fertilizer for personal development, spawning opportunity when it is least expected.

Clever and astute, he sacrifices immediate gratification for long-term security. He holds the key to measured awareness and the ability to use this wisdom to further his plans for the future.

By remaining grounded and focused, he can rely on his intuition to guide him to many completed projects. Each plan continues to be measured, checked, and rechecked for a solid launch.

Each accomplishment adds to his confidence and supplies him with the multi-dimensional aspects that further his creativity.

Defeat is not in his vocabulary. He upholds the banner of success as if his life depended on it; in his humble world, it does. He is the harbinger of change who knows that a new infrastructure must be set as the old structure falls.

Step into Developing Energy and Become the Prince of Disks:

The Prince of Disks is the Architect who thrives on environmental challenges that rely on careful planning. He is the Designing Earth Energy that challenges you to exist entirely in the material world.

He understands that substantial accomplishments depend upon determination, courage, and the willingness to sacrifice to achieve.

Imagine yourself holding your entire future in your hands with the ability to create anything you desire through hard work. You establish the groundwork for the future through the source of your strength: resourceful knowledge.

As the Prince of Disks, you accept the challenge to SEE, to align yourself with authentic achievement.

It is a time to take stock of your internal maturation. Years of careful planning now demand physical action, and the sensation of security is stripped away. You can no longer rely upon others. Your destiny is in your own hands.

Once you realize you command the force that propels you forward, destructive influences lurk in the shadows. Doubt is ready to creep in, cloud your judgment, and undermine your evolution. The old guard continues to nag that what once was should still exist.

You know better. Your innate sense of direction shields you from the status quo that would shift your path. Claiming authority over your decisions allows a clear view of your design and brings about self-assurance.

Through a stringent policy of continued progress, you note the aspects necessary to survival: health, strength, agility, and renewable energy.

You take the trials and tribulations of life and use the momentum to rebuild and regenerate. Though there is a sense of danger, you charge ahead despite it, declaring yourself undefeated.

You can begin the renovation by taking a hard and often harsh look at the materials you've used to construct your physical world. You can change your methods if you do not like what you see in the whole light of day.

The dynamic outline you created to catapult you toward your goals allows you to create a unique measuring stick for the future. With careful planning, the old growth can be pruned, plucked, and reshaped into what you know is your true form.

Your physical presence demands a strong foundation - without the established base, you cannot expand to your total capacity. There is much more than you know about yourself.

The Prince of Disks offers the opportunity to recognize and act upon building practical and sustainable structures filled with love and graceful details. The grand structure starts from the inside. Design your future through careful consideration.

Prince of Disks' Mantra:

"I seek the right pattern for success, recognizing I depend on my creativity. I am the guide to future achievement."

The Heart Of Tarot
Questions from the Prince of Disks:

- How do you build a strong foundation?

- What physical inventory is available to you?

- How does careful planning catapult you forward?

- What allows you to embrace your authentic achievements?

- What is your source of renewable energy?

- What gives you the strength to create reliable boundaries?

- What stubborn behavior blinds you to fresh growth?

- How do you maintain patience while building a new foundation?

- What feeds your soul during the reconstruction?

- How do you expose your vulnerability?

Dr. Ruth A. Souther

PRINCE OF CUPS
(Passionate Heart)

EMOTIONAL TRANSFORMATION
EXPRESSIVE DESIRE
HEALTHY RELATIONSHIPS
INNOVATIVE HEIGHTS
SPIRITUALLY HEALED

Astrology Note: Water of Water—River
Archetype: The Sage

The Prince of Cups represents the challenge of having a true **emotional transformation** by releasing and healing sacred wounds. The Prince of Cups is the ability to convert the pain of the past into a joyous and passionate heart.

You can be deeply devoted and moved to such **expressive desire** in your relationships that you immerse yourself in the murky depths of irresistible overcompensation. Giving too much often feels good but leads to complicated relationships.

By recognizing past patterns, you can rise above the swamp and regain healthy relationships with yourself and those around you. As a spiritually healed and mature adult, you can soar to innovative heights by allowing an empathic understanding of your true feelings. You can choose healthy relationships and ignore the ways of the past by embracing the depths of your passion.

The Prince of Cups' shadow understands you could indulge yourself with the idea of being a wounded romantic and become an emotional vampire. The tendency to be dramatic and delusional leads to more rejection and self-pity as you doom yourself to repeat the patterns of an unstable heart.

Your empathy turns to passive resistance, and you suffer at your own hands as you wallow in the swamp of self-destructive behavior. You could reach a point of emotional suicide that leaves you cold, unfeeling, detached, and vindictive. The romantic notion of embracing a sacred wound as a way of life is detrimental to the whole heart.

The Prince of Cups' challenge is to be the Sage who expands upon the intuitive cycles the Mystic Princess began by creating a pattern of waves to wash ashore the necessary debris.

It is all good to immerse yourself in the **sentimental depths** of desire, yet there comes a point when getting lost in the muck is easy.

He expresses the need for **emotional balance** and thus becomes the yardstick by which the internal and external pressure is measured. He encourages heartfelt evaluations and clears the way for a detached perspective that establishes equilibrium.

Healthy and attentive, he interacts with the people and events in his life with the understanding there is a time to retreat, review, restructure, and reorder. He can guard against harmful emotional exposure and guide the way through the darkest times.

Controlling his emotions with a tolerant view toward the motives behind his feelings becomes his most significant test. Knowledge and self-awareness are the keywords to his success: knowing the source of his pain and incorporating that awareness into the healing process.

Unlike the Princess, who swims beneath the surface, the Prince must learn detachment to shift the growing tidal wave in his favor. He must learn to surf the curling edges to safety or risk drowning in his emotions.

Step into Developing Energy and Become the Prince of Cups:

The Prince of Disks is the Architect who thrives on receptive, emotional expeditions that reveal the true nature of your wounds. He is the Designing Water Energy that provides a detailed assessment of the problematic past that will offer you the courage to face the present. He understands you can heal from a soul level by uncovering and examining the pain.

Imagine yourself with the ability to fly, to be able to view your emotional landscape from above. This bird's eye view gives you the power to see the murky waters ahead that threaten to blind you.

You can see the obstructions that divert your true desires, and with this victory, you become strong and capable, no longer a victim of circumstance.

As the Prince of Cups, you accept the challenge to FEEL, embrace the wound, and endorse healing.

You reflect a vast range of sentiments in overwhelming sensations at any moment. Some pass by as a momentary distraction, while others create a predicament where you could quickly lose yourselves in the murky depths.

To rise above the dangers of maudlin histrionics, you must come to terms with your true feelings. Inner stability is achieved once you face those thoughts, ideas, and realities head-on.

When you rise above the dilemmas with a different perspective, you gain control of your emotions and present a united front. The possibilities flow past this fresh and heartfelt place, and you choose how to react to these tests.

Rather than being sucked into a hurricane of unrestrained theatrics, you maintain your distance, thereby establishing a core value of discernment. You become realistic and stable, reminding yourself that even the tiniest detail if missed, can make the best-laid plan go awry and create emotional hazards.

The Prince of Cups offers the opportunity to recognize and act upon the release of psychic damage, which will heal internal grief. Give up the murky depths for sunshine. Rise above the emotional drama and see a new perspective.

Prince of Cups Mantra:

"I analyze each layer of my emotional excavation from a logical, and therefore, detached perspective, thereby defining myself as the guide to confidence and strength."

The Heart Of Tarot

Questions from the Prince of Cups:

- How do you release old emotional patterns?

- When have you indulged the wounded romantic?

- How do you embrace your passion?

- What takes you to innovative heights?

- How does self-indulgent behavior throw you out of emotional balance?

- How do you reach the sentimental depths necessary to access the source of your wounding?

- Where in your life does a detached perspective serve you best?

- What unacknowledged pain stops your ability to encourage indorsed healing?

- What is your greatest asset that strengthens you to establish emotional inner stability?

Dr. Ruth A. Souther

Expanding Energy:

The KNIGHT

The Heart Of Tarot

The Knight reviews the visionary concepts now drawn into the blueprints of the future. He takes a careful and concentrated look at the plans and begins the expansion. What was merely a dream and two-dimensional idea drawn out of the chaos of life is now in the process of becoming a sturdy structure.

The possibilities are endless. By initiating change, The Knight brings the dream to reality. He leaps forward with fiery intent, knowing his leadership will bring forth the revisionists within his troops. He calls the sun to boil away fear and allow consciousness to become a reality. Transformation occurs only with a leap of faith.

The Knight advocates for those who have lost their way, directs attention to the next level of intuition, casts the stones upon the waters of confusion, and becomes the heart's defender. As he advances, he shapeshifts into the Shaman, the bridge between above and below: Intuition and Awareness.

Action is necessary to succeed. Reviewing long ago experiences brings the lessons forward, which become the building blocks for success. Integrity is critical to learning what went wrong and what will work. There are no lies within the domain of the Knight—the plan can always be altered if honesty is primary when planning the ongoing path.

The Knight knows when to draw back. To push forward when ego is the driving force, emotion is high, or hurtful words are ready to spew forth is the path to destruction. Stand still. Be patient. Observe. Detach. Wait for the right moment.

His energy connects to the harvest season when life reaches fulfillment. It is the gathering time when crops mature, and he reaps what he sows. He understands consequences and penalties can be high when one takes the difficult road of truthfulness and honor within himself. He has no choice but to do the right thing.

The Knight is the Champion. He is the Heat, the Authority, the Foundation, and the Oceanic Mysteries. He is the Builder who constructs the future. His action is to take raw material and turn it into concrete achievements.

Archetypically speaking, he is the Advocate who lights the fire, the Warrior who continues the growth process, the Champion who battles for justice, and the Prophet who knows the outcome.

The Expanding Knight says, "What if my structures disappoint, and I crash upon the shores of failure?"

His Mother, the Queen, says, "Oh, but my Darling, what if you succeed? What if you build the future?"

A Builder constructs the future.

Dr. Ruth A. Souther

Questions from the Knight

- What blueprint reflects your current plan of action?

- What dream is ready to expand?

- When have you lost your way?

- How do you access your instinctual path?

- How will you know it's the right moment to build?

- What is your integrity based on?

- How do you find fulfillment?

- How do you advocate for yourself?

- What is the most significant consequence of change?

- What energy do you draw upon to build your dream?

The Heart Of Tarot

KNIGHT OF WANDS
(Energetic Transformation)

RELIABLE VIEWPOINT
ENERGETIC TRANSFORMATION
INNOVATIVE GROWTH
INTERNAL PERSPECTIVE
UNDENIABLE GRACE

Astrology Note: Air of Fire—Heat
Archetype: The Advocate

The Knight of Wands represents the challenge to accept the fiery revelations brought about by an internal vision quest. The Knight of Wands is the ability to uphold daring ideals for **energetic transformation** through a **reliable viewpoint**.

By recognizing your talents, you can embrace your dreams and accept the emotional fulfillment of **innovative growth**. You discover you must take action on the ideas springing into your awareness. No longer content to daydream about the future, you are motivated to transform, change, grow, and become everything you have always wanted to be.

Take action on the power stemming from a profound shift of **internal perspective** regarding who you are and what you want. You are ready to shed old beliefs and patterns that have held you back, and you now ride into a state of victory.

The Knight of Wands' shadow knows it is possible to become a bully as you focus too intently on your desires. It is easy to forget how your actions affect those around you. The rush you get when you achieve your goals could lead to running roughshod right over those who disagree with you.

In that same rush, you might lose sight of your true nature and evolve into fakery. You could move from showmanship into show-off status, creating discord and disenfranchisement while those around you dismiss your reckless behavior. You may hurry so quickly to the end that you forget that most of the pleasure is in the journey.

The Knight of Wands' challenge is to be the advocate who shares his experience with the world. He is independent and allows no limits on his fortune. The possibilities are endless as he surges forward and brings a rush of heat to soften the inevitable denial of potential.

His torch is Olympian, the symbol of conquest whose nature rivals no one. He rides into the storm, confident of success and willing to sacrifice—or make sacred—the truth of his existence.

The Knight understands there will be trial and error, missed moments, and mistakes along the route. The challenge of rising above the chaos and listening to his instincts is strong. He is a warrior whose intuitive nature guides him forward without fail.

Step into Energy and become the Knight of Wands:

As the moon begins to withdraw, the shadows lengthen. You have a heightened sense of awareness that time is running out, and although you are no longer afraid of the darkness that reaches toward you. You can't help the backward glance. Have you done all that you came here to do?

Have you led a meaningful existence? Have you made significant strides in your ideology? Have you allowed yourself to mature, expand, and accept those thoughts that drove you forward?

Or did you put up a good fight, denying your place in the world, turning back to the childish set of standards you once held? Look now at the structures you've built and the foundations you created, and view them from a detached place of grounded illumination. See the flaws of your conception, the downfall of your desires, and the fabricated reality you surrounded yourself with to survive.

Find and cling to that sense of humor. You will need it as you progress further into your intuitive selves. Personal power cannot be purchased; it can only be earned through hard work, dedication, and authentic behavior. Actions speak louder than mere words.

Personal power is not bestowed upon you in a ceremony but creeps up and overtakes you by surprise while you are in the trenches. You are imbued with an intense energy that feels right and good. You find your true nature just before the moon hides once again from your sight.

The Knight of Wands offers the opportunity to recognize and act upon the inspiration and focus of burning away obstacles in the path to success. By extending the flame of potential out into the world, the Universe supplies <u>undeniable grace.</u>

Knight of Wands Mantra:

"I know my talents and benefits as well as my faults and weaknesses. I go forward in acceptance of my true self."

Questions from the Knight of Wands:

- **What talent brings growth possibilities?**

- How do you lose sight of your goals?

- **What motivates you to victory?**

- What is your most significant flaw?

- **What is your greatest gift?**

- When have you lost sight of your intuition?

- **What do you identify as a meaningful existence?**

- How did you survive a setback?

- **When have you denied your gifts?**

- How do you charge forward with this new perspective?

Dr. Ruth A. Souther

KNIGHT OF SWORDS
(Focused Mind)

ENLIGHTENED PURPOSE
ENERGETIC AMBITION
DEDICATED DETERMINATION
RECEPTIVE COMPASSION
ASSERTIVE COMMUNICATION

Astrology Note: Air of Air—Authority
Archetype: The Warrior

The Knight of Swords represents the challenge to communicate with the passion of committed intentions brought about by a focused mind. The Knight of Swords is the ability to go forward with **enlightened purpose** infused with sacred ideology.

The emancipation achieved through the actions of a liberated mind has brought you a sense of **energetic ambition** and **dedicated determination** to carry through with your goals. You become a dynamic force of nature when you combine emotional depth with the intellectual process to create a focused, passionate thought process.

You hold the duality of **receptive compassion** and **assertive communication** in your hands as you ride into the winds of change. You discover that balancing the opposite ends of the spectrum gives profound intensity and meaning to the ideals you have set for yourself.

The Knight of Swords' shadow understands you may become exhausted with the energetic effort to succeed if you do not maintain a sense of grounded energy. You may fly high with exhilaration as your mind becomes free. You may sail along on an emotional feeling of satisfaction, but if you do not take care, you may crash into the cliffs of overachievement.

You risk becoming headstrong and stubborn as the fascination with your cleverness takes hold. You may start irrelevant arguments to hear yourself talk. You could miss the minor connections and the small details that make up the bigger picture because you are too enamored of your talents.

The Knight of Swords' challenge is to be the Warrior who holds truth and justice as his weapons of choice. Without heartfelt honesty and fairness, there is no path forward. He soars through the air on his steed—which doubles for his intuition—and moves toward higher perception.

He can look at life from a different perspective and each situation from all sides of thought. His sense of integrity drives him to question, research, and seek answers from every source available. He can justly hear all aspects of the discussion by not taking a specific opinion to heart.

The Knight understands he is not the judge and jury but the witness of the unfolding dramas and chooses to rise above pettiness while feeling the tragic qualities of those who plead for mercy. He knows very well that life is a double-sided coin, and there is no right or wrong, just passions of the heart. He uses his mind to detach and step back. It is not his job to decide who wins or loses.

Step into Energy and become the Knight of Swords:

The moon pulls into a crescent, shrinking in on itself as if deep in thought, wishing to be undisturbed as it ponders the tales of old. The warm nights stir recollections of your stories, bringing to mind the lessons you presented along your path. To estimate your progress and how far you've come over the years, evaluate your actions through grounded meditation.

Reach far inside. Look for structure and foundations that keep you honest. Perhaps you strayed from that model. Maybe that arrangement no longer works—whatever the reality is, be bold, be truthful.

Where have you been? Where are you now? Where are you headed? The future is unclear, but you can determine the best possible choices through careful analysis.

You are a composite of the millions of tiny decisions you've made. Sometimes, the picture is a brilliant mixture of color and texture, expressing exactly what you wanted. More likely, the view is duller, less viable, and dissatisfying.

Why? Because you deem yourselves both judge and jury in the harshest sense. During this time of inward processing, you must find a way to congratulate yourself on a job well done. You survived the worst and are alive, prepared for the next adventure. Turn away from disappointment in things that you cannot change. Turn toward new standards of thought that bring growth and psychological development.

The Knight of Swords offers the opportunity to recognize and act upon communication with truthful compassion. Staying balanced and allowing all possible perceptions to be in the discussion is essential. Focused energy brings excellent strides toward the future.

The Knight of Swords mantra:

"I know my limitations and ambitions are exhausting, but my perceptions are balanced and real. I go forward with purpose and communicate my needs."

Dr. Ruth A. Souther

Questions from the Knight of Swords:

- Where do you find yourself exhausted with the effort of appearances?

- What is your biggest disappointment?

- What minor but important detail needs your awareness?

- What balance is between emotional response and intellectual approach?

- What allows you to communicate your feelings with intention?

- What is your greatest disappointment?

- What is your current reality?

- What is the basis for your psychological development?

- How do you view the future?

- What symbolizes your progress?

- When have you harshly judged yourself?

- How do you focus your energy?

The Heart Of Tarot

KNIGHT OF DISKS
(Prosperous Boundaries)

MANIFEST ABUNDANCE
PRACTICAL KNOWLEDGE
PHYSICAL HEALING
WEALTHY PROFUSION
SUSTAINED COURAGE

Astrology Note: Air of Earth—Defender
Archetype: The Champion

The Knight of Disks represents the challenge to **manifest abundance** through focused methodical work. The Knight of Disks is the ability to provide a safe and secure space to construct creative aspirations brought about by prosperous boundaries.

You have prepared the way by being self-responsible and diligent in your efforts to protect the established limits of your resources. The foundations you labored over now provide you with the ability to nourish you in the future. The question is, are you strong enough to collect your reward?

The **practical knowledge** that sustained you during the difficult times, the creative abilities you nurtured throughout the droughts, the **physical healing** you fought for, the emotional growth you endured—all of it has grown from seeds into a **wealthy profusion** that is ripe and ready to pick. Take action and find the **sustained courage** to collect the rich return that belongs to you. You must be prepared for battle to safeguard your talents.

The Knight of Disks' shadow knows you may not have the fortitude to take what rightfully belongs to you. There is always external pressure to give up what is earned. Be aware some prefer to take rather than give. If you are not careful, you may relinquish your harvest to bullies.

You have a strong body, mind, heart, and soul, but, at times, you must retreat from the battle. You may feel disloyal if you argue with family or friends and become helpless in your anger. Your hard work could disappear right in front of your eyes. You must learn to be assertive, stand your ground, and fight when necessary.

The Knight of Disks' challenge is to be the Champion and know which dragons are real or imagined. It's not about ego or greed. It is about his honor and how he protected his Queen. He stands his ground, waiting for dawn so he can view his world in the light. He knows darkness can be deceiving, distorting, and disorienting. He must see the direction he faces by the sun's brightness and become conscious of every detail.

He works within the boundaries he created as a pact with Earth to sustain both, as all living things are symbiotic with the land. His 'dragons' represent his choices, regrets, and successes—the moments of triumph and when he chose to step back. There is no shame in refusing to fight, especially if the clash is petty and unproductive.

The Knight understands patience is a virtue. He stands ready to do battle, but only if threatened. Wisdom and experience guide his decisions; he will not move until he is confident it is correct. He resists rash actions that undermine his goals of peace and security within his ranks. He is solid and demands respect from a united perspective.

Step into Energy and become the Knight of Disks:

The Earth is still green, but beneath the foliage, you know things are changing. The Moon is a waning crescent, still brilliant against the night sky. Soon, it will disappear. Now, you must ask yourself whether you have followed your original intention.

This phase of your life was about restructuring, rebuilding, and discovering new foundations out of the rubble from your past. You must now define the materials you will use for the final construction. What does your ethical makeup look like? Will you take shortcuts, refuse to review your mistakes, and possibly use unstable ideas to build upon?

Or will you choose a mature and grounded process to eliminate faulty production? Your creative choices today deeply impact the conclusions you draw to face the future.

This is your chance to make good on everything that has occurred in your lifetime. You must balance somewhere between good or bad, positive or negative. You cannot afford to dismiss actions, however painful. You must, instead, repair and reinforce the lessons to build a durable structure that will remain for the rest of your lives.

The defects remind us that nothing and no one is perfect. All those decisions were based on what you knew at the time. You can choose to be enlightened and productive, incorporating these difficulties into your structure, or you can ignore past challenges and risk an earthquake that will bring it all down.

The Heart Of Tarot

The Knight of Disks offers the opportunity to recognize and act upon the art of conservation. Learning to preserve and protect the resources that nourish the future is an art form. The physical body is a canvas ready to transform.

Knight of Disks Mantra:

"I know I am not perfect, and my boundaries are often tested, yet I am patient and willing to battle for the right cause."

Questions from the Knight of Disks:

- When have you felt helpless to protect your boundaries?

- How have you given away your rightful harvest?

- What provides physical healing?

- How do you become responsible for your prosperity?

- When have you been unstable?

- What feeds your productivity?

- What is the foundation of your ethics?

- How do you balance the past with the present?

- What promise have you made to support your goals?

- Is that promise still viable, or is it ready to be released?

The Heart Of Tarot

KNIGHT OF CUPS
(Loyal Heart)

EXPANDED GENEROSITY
MOTIVATED TRUST
TOLERANT INDIVIDUAL
EMOTIONAL CONNECTION
POSITIVE CHANGES

Astrology Note: Air of Water—Ocean
Archetype: The Prophet

The Knight of Cups represents the challenge to willingly commit to an **expanded generosity** of shared emotions by accepting that perfection is a myth. The Knight of Cups is the ability to embrace a loyal heart despite failed expectations.

Ride forward with an open heart and **motivated trust** to triumph over the pain of disappointment. Accept the role of a **tolerant individual** who regards devotion as an assurance of love. You can bring an **emotional connection** beyond ego and vanity when you understand that compassion is a form of unconditional love.

Once you become aware of how your feelings affect others, you make decisions based on empathy. After riding through the storm generated by awareness and insights into the sentimental depths of your loyalties, you are equipped to draw new lines of defense. Offer love without reluctance and yet recognize dangerously tight boundaries. You will see the **positive changes** mirrored within the psyche.

The Knight of Cups' shadow understands you could lose sight of your boundaries and become an emotional vampire, feeding off others to keep yourself in a place of power. You must remember you will get back what you put into the world.

Love and Light, if only superficially offered, may ultimately harm you. You can also become a victim to others who would take advantage of your tolerance. It is a delicate balance between being emotionally available while protecting your trust and loyalty against misuse by devious people.

The Knight of Cups' challenge is to be the Prophet, who foresees the future and acts accordingly. He rides with his arms outstretched to welcome the diversity and shifting of his emotional needs. His intuition guides him to seek security within the boundaries of his heart and not react to the drama of those around him.

He remembers it is often difficult to maintain distance when sentiment is involved.

He flies upward for perspective and sees many paths forward if he guards his feelings against the onslaught of his emotional borders.

The Knight of Cups' challenge is to be available yet not give everything away until he is drained and exhausted. He connects to the divine energy of all that exists to support him in eliminating the emotions that are not his. What belongs to him, and what does not?

Step into Energy and become the Knight of Cups:

The moon shrinks to a thin sliver, ready to disappear once again from your sight. You recognize the cycles in nature, the same ones reflected in your life. There are times of significant gain and terrible loss; there is abundance and drought.

Your emotional waters are muddied and murky, but a good, cleansing rain clears the way to health and happiness. Your well-being depends on the ability to purge the past of guilt and remorse. Once you have acknowledged the wounding, you must see how to dismantle the obstructions that cause you to cling to it.

Call these obstacles by name, hold them up to the light, and examine them from different perspectives. Why are they there? Why can't you let it go? You know these wounds no longer serve. You no longer cling to these wounds as victims of circumstance. You want them to go away. Why don't they? What else can you do?

The blame is locked deep inside every wound, however irrational and ridiculous it might seem. From early childhood, you have faulted yourself for your behavior. If you did not cause the pain directly, you must have contributed to it.

Even when it seems impossible to have done so, if you dig deep enough, you will find this sentiment to be true. You can no longer be content to count the ways you are damaged. You must take action from a grounded and stable place of emotional maturity. You must reach out and embrace forgiveness. Yes, you must forgive those who have hurt you, but along that path, you discover the most critical realization of all: you must first forgive yourself.

The Knight of Cups offers the opportunity to recognize and act upon the protection of an open heart by becoming an emotional warrior who defends the power of love at all costs. Generosity is a state of being, and happiness descends like a once-achieved mantle.

The Knight of Cups Mantra:

"The truth of my heart awaits discovery. There is no rush to decide which direction I need to go. I guard my emotional healing as a vital step to wholeness."

Questions from the Knight of Cups:

- Where do you give away your emotional power?

- How do you let go of the idea that you must be perfect?

- What allows you to accept yourself for who you truly are?

- How do you create boundaries and yet remain emotionally available?

- What obstructs your path?

- How do you release those obstacles?

- How do you purge the painful past?

- How do you complete this cycle?

- What is the way to self-forgiveness?

- How do you make honest emotional connections?

Dr. Ruth A. Souther

SUMMONING ENERGY:

THE QUEEN

The Heart Of Tarot

The Queen summons all possibilities within her command. She holds the keys to the Princesses' dreams of destiny and supports the Princes' design. She finances the materials for the Knights to build future structures. All things flow from her generosity as she fiercely protects her Queendom.

She is the epitome of the natural world, the embodiment of the elements of fire, wind, earth, and water. She radiates the raw power of wildfires, tornados, earthquakes, and tsunamis to shake the defenses put in place to block growth. She understands the spiral path of evolution and the desire for humanity to succeed.

The Queen is the definition of ethics—everything she represents is for the moral awareness of humankind. She stands in her power to guide divine illumination into the physical world. She is aware the experiences of the past weigh heavily on the present, and until reconciliation is achieved, the future remains murky.

She is not without her lessons. She knows every occurrence is a valuable opportunity to define her spiritual truth. The Queen never forgets where she came from, the paths she has traveled, or the mistakes she made while on that same path.

She remembers every detail of the chaos while sorting out what belongs to her and what does not. A rational assessment of her thoughts brings harmony to her emotional truth. Once her mind and heart agree, she can remove the martyr mask and step back from the disturbing quagmire of feelings. Only then can she truly see who she is and what her next incarnation will be.

The Queen is the Summoner. She is the magic of desire and manifestation. She engages intuition and sentiment. She calls forth the evolution of the soul. The Queen is always the Queen in any deck. She remains the constant reminder of reclaiming personal empowerment.

Archetypically speaking, she is the Activator who propels the energy forward, the Foundation that supports the changes, the Mobilizer who creates the opportunities, and the Psychic who takes ownership of the project and oversees the process.

The Summoning Queen says, "What if I lose my way and my children suffer for my inconsistencies?"

Her higher Self says, "Oh, but my Darling, what if you find the way? What if you create the safety necessary for their growth?"

A Summoner calls forth action.

Questions from the Queen:

- What represents your ethics?

- How do you sort out the chaos in your life?

- How does your generosity support you?

- What does your divine connection tell you?

- How do you embody the natural world?

- How do you manifest ownership?

- What is your spiritual truth?

- How do you remove your martyr's mask?

- Where does your magic come from?

- How do you summon your power?

The Heart Of Tarot

QUEEN OF WANDS
(Radiant Transformation)

FEARLESS VISION
INTUITIVE KNOWLEDGE
ACTIVE REVOLUTION
SPIRITUAL AWAKENING
LUMINOUS VALOR

Astrology Note: Fire of Fire—Wildfire
Archetype: The Activator

The Queen of Wands represents the challenge of mastering authentic identity by allowing self-awareness to drive radiant transformation. The Queen of Wands is the ability to recreate the universe through a fearless vision of the future.

Trusting in the newly discovered **intuitive knowledge** you gained during an **active revolution** against old ideas is a novel concept. The courage of your hard-earned convictions has replaced the preconceived notions that prevented you from a spiritual awakening.

Once you truly believe in yourself, you can envision yourself whole. When you can face your worst fear and shine the light of luminous valor on those things that eat away at your self-confidence, you can become the master of your destiny. Realizing you have complete authority over your psychic energy, you know anything is possible. Personal power is in your hands.

The Queen of Wands' shadow can become overbearing and arrogant in this newfound awareness. Your way is the right way, the only way, and all other views are dismissed as conjecture rather than the valid views of others who have found their way through the fires of transformation.

If you do not take care, you could become a self-righteous dictator, forcing your views on others. You cannot afford to turn away from your fears as they act as a guide to past lessons. Instead, keep those fears by your side as a constant reminder of how far you have come.

The Queen of Wands' challenge is a relationship with the Wildfire that ignites her authentic personality. She brings the energy to transform even the gentlest push into creative awareness. She sits upon her throne, looking through a perspective gained by trial and error, never forgetting how she achieved her success.

Mistakes were made, but the moral guidance of higher intuition brought her back to her path of activation. She admits the lessons and does not hesitate to reconcile with the past. The only way to move forward is to burn away the old and allow the new to grow.

The Queen of Wands' challenge is maintaining her integrity while engaging in authentic action. Ego could destroy all she built if she is not careful to reassess her path. She is the Activator. She inspires courage, confidence, and creativity to live life fully without regret.

Step into Destiny and become the Queen of Wands:

The moon is at the height of her glory, full and round, bright with promise, a cold, shining beacon pointed at your path. You stand momentarily, wholly aware of the stark contrast of light and shadow before and behind us. You are between the worlds, past, and future, entirely in the present.

You weigh your actions, thoughts, feelings, and integrity. Now is the time to reconcile with the past, learn from mistakes, heal wounds, and allow mistrial to guide you toward wholeness. Forgiveness for past errors is vital for your growth. Forgiveness removes the stumbling blocks. Forgiveness is divine intervention.

Divine illumination is offered to help you find your way in the world. You are led to your true purpose by opening to enlightenment. When you look outward and take stock of all you have ever been, you get a glimpse of all you can be. To accept this challenging path, you must clearly define yourself and what you accept as your truth.

Honesty is represented by moral awareness: how you behave in the social circle, among friends and family, is the guiding light. You must open yourselves to the wisdom of the ages and hold yourselves to the highest standards to make progress.

The Queen of Wands offers the opportunity to take self-confident action by embracing the courage of convictions that comes with spiritual awakening. Walking through fire brings strength of character; accept and own the impossible.

The Queen of Wands' Mantra:

"I know every second of life is a defining moment, an opportunity to grow spiritually. I go forward with integrity, in search of a better world."

The Heart Of Tarot

Questions from the Queen of Wands:

- What past issue prevents you from achieving in the present?

- When has self-righteous behavior dictated your actions?

- How do you embrace courage?

- What energy allows radiant transformation?

- How do you become whole and self-confident?

- How do you reconcile the past with the present?

- What is the key to your forgiveness?

- What is your moral truth?

- When has your ego taken control?

- What action is necessary to regain your integrity?

Dr. Ruth A. Souther

QUEEN OF SWORDS
(Observing Mind)

BALANCED PROCESS
TRUE IDENTITY
INTELLECTUAL CLARITY
ANALYTICAL COMMUNICATOR
OBJECTIVE DISCERNMENT

Astrology Note: Fire of Air—Tornado
Archetype: The Mobilizer

The Queen of Swords represents the challenge to establish a profoundly objective and **balanced process** of thought based on an observing mind. The Queen of Swords is the ability to logically calculate and remove obstacles that block the path to success.

You become the master of your **true identity** when you cut away the resistance that masks your **intellectual clarity**. When you use your gift as the **analytical communicator**, you become the defender of logic who uses words to heal wounds and create harmony.

You can examine your faults from a detached state of mind and achieve far beyond the pressures of the past. You see the patterns established with an **objective discernment** that allows you to deepen your awareness, grow, and evolve into a higher consciousness. You seek truth, clarity, and authenticity from this place within your thoughts and words.

The Queen of Swords' shadow could develop an unsympathetic and somewhat harsh manner of communication simply because you believe you know best. Your ideas become the most critical driving force behind your actions, which could manifest in an inflated sense of self-worth.

Impatience and cutting words become habits despite the hurt you inflict on others. At this point, it is easy to become unreasonable as you justify your behavior. You lose sight of the power behind the spoken word and lash out if you feel your control slipping away.

The Queen of Swords' challenge is to remove the martyr mask from herself before accusing anyone else of holding back. When she hid from her wounds, she lost her identity until she embraced an honest evaluation of her past. Rather than actively fight the changes, she acknowledges how evolution has shaped her truth.

Her energy is a tornado of thoughts, concepts, disagreements, and self-criticism threatening to destroy her if she does not fight for her truth. She steps into her power once she assesses her goals and releases the denial of things that cannot be changed.

The Queen of Swords embraces this new perspective shift and transforms into a powerhouse that functions without disarming others. She becomes the Mobilizer, calling forth her troops to find a peaceful solution to the war within.

Step into Destiny and become the Queen of Swords:

The full moon rides high in the sky, barely discernable in the daytime, visible only as a white, translucent orb. It holds the hope of a new season of growth and awareness. The moon appears as if in a dream, there, and yet, not there, just like your thoughts that are clear and concise one moment and then hidden in a cloud of doubt the next.

The challenge is to find a coherent process to sort out the details that cause self-doubt. Why did I do that? Why did I make that decision? How did I miss that? What made me do that? It is human nature to focus on the negative rather than the positive. Still, it is precisely that motivation that should drive you to find reasonable resolutions, which leads to constructive reinforcement.

For this open and honest appraisal, you must allow a connection to your higher consciousness. This place will enable you to detach from emotional investment and evaluate yourselves from a divine point of view. Then, you will see the complete picture.

You must step away from the issues to find clarity. It takes courage to rationally assess your needs versus your desires and find the stamina to discover what you truly want versus what you think you should do.

Who told you to feel like that? Who said this is what you should do? Where did those ideas come from? Why did you embrace that particular suggestion? Strip away what does not belong to you and discover what makes you whole.

The Queen of Swords offers the opportunity to recognize and act upon a defense of logic, to cut away unnecessary ideas, and to focus on mental clarity. Trust that when the truth is revealed, one is empowered and capable of changing the world. A focused mind can cause a revolution.

The Queen of Swords' Mantra:

"I can follow through no matter how difficult things become. I persevere to the end despite the many obstacles in my path."

Questions from the Queen of Swords:

- What mask hides you from the truth?

- When has your behavior been unreasonable?

- What gives you the strength to communicate objectively?

- How do you accept the power of your mind?

- What belief inhibits you?

- What logic drives you?

- What does your higher consciousness tell you?

- How do you conduct an honest evaluation?

- When have you been in denial of past decisions?

- How do you step into your truth?

The Heart Of Tarot

QUEEN OF DISKS
(Sanctioned Boundaries)

**CONNECTED AWARENESS
PHYSICAL AUTHORITY
SIGNIFICANT POWER
TANGIBLE CONFIDENCE
CLEAR AFFIRMATION**

**Astrology Note: Fire of Earth—Earthquake
Archetype: The Guardian**

The Queen of Disks represents the challenge to forge a path of **connected awareness** to the material world. The Queen of Disks is the ability to be grounded, peaceful, and resourceful while retaining **physical authority** over sanctioned boundaries.

You become the master of your destiny when you take the time to look at where you have been and assess where you are going before moving forward. You become a self-fulfilling prophecy when you exercise significant power over your life. No one else controls your path. You alone can regenerate yourself over and over.

You provide the **tangible confidence** to feed your mind, heart, body, and soul connection. You engineer, design, and build the world you want to live in as you create a new awareness of your abilities. You have **clear affirmation** that provides security and quality for this life. Your future belongs to you; you must face it with pride, dignity, and a new-found sense of freedom.

The Queen of Disks' shadow becomes tedious and without imagination if you get caught up in the riches you have discovered. Your belief in yourself means resting on your laurels and the fruits of your labor. You become decadent and possibly exploitative when you lose sight of your journey and forget the desert you traveled through to reach the oasis.

If you look only upon your accumulated wealth, you may forget your past or the lessons you learned. Those experiences created the foundation of wisdom, allowing you to evolve into a higher consciousness.

The Queen of Disks' challenge is to embrace her experiences and acknowledge every whim and wandering path that brought her to the summit of achievement. As she ponders the road to success, it is essential to understand that each disappointment and difficulty was preparation to become the foundation upon which to grow.

She takes a moment to relish her triumphs, knowing her internal fortitude kept her going through the desert of depression. When hard times hit, she takes up her staff and keeps moving forward despite wanting to quit. Every earthquake was a wake-up call, propelling her into the future.

The Queen of Disks is the Guardian who holds the keys to the future. She does not accept opposition from her inner arguments, as she has seen the devastation caused by her resistance to change. She steps forward with confidence and supplies a foundation for building the future.

Step into the Divine and become the Queen of Disks:

The air is hot and still, insects buzz around, crickets chirp, and the Earth is lush and blooming. When the full moon rises, it appears magnified—a vast, glowing orb suspended in the sky. Shadows are in deep contrast to the brightly lit landscape. The difference between the two becomes a familiar metaphor for life.

Externally, your landscape is illuminated, and as you stumble toward awareness, you hope for the best outcome. Internally, much is cast in darkness: your power and positive reinforcement are locked away, out of reach. The secrets to your success lie within those shadows, as they are lessons that should not be forgotten.

Do not deceive yourself into forgetting the past. Embrace both aspects of yourself and find the physical balance between light and dark to reach the point of divine maturation. When you can stand on the border between the two aspects, you can apply practical solutions to your problems.

You are the engineer of your future. Where you build and how you build is solely in your control. Learn from your mistakes rather than hiding them deep within your psyche to emerge when least expected. If you practice sound architecture, you become the master of your future rather than a servant to the past.

The Queen of Disks offers the challenge of building a new physical reality by remembering the difficult roads traveled. Remember why this route was chosen. Never forget the path of the past as it forges the future.

Queen of Disks' mantra:"

I examined all that was to learn and build new and improved structures to support my goals. I will forgive my faults and make them my strengths."

The Heart Of Tarot

Questions from the Queen of Disks:

- What part of your past is ready to examine?

- How do you detach from your history?

- What allows you to see a bright future?

- What affirmation provides safety and security?

- How do you regenerate from past wounds?

- How do you rebuild your freedom?

- How do you give your power away?

- What brings you to awareness?

- What is your greatest deception?

- What is the foundation to build the future?

Dr. Ruth A. Souther

QUEEN OF CUPS
(Authentic Heart)

**UNCONDITIONAL LOVE
TOLERANT PERSPECTIVE
SPOKEN TRUTH
EXPRESSIVE AFFECTION
EMOTIONAL HEALING**

**Astrology Note: Fire of Water—Tsunami
Archetype: The Psychic**

The Queen of Cups represents the challenge of having an authentic heart while giving birth to new and mature concepts involving emotional relationships. The Queen of Cups can express **unconditional love** from a **tolerant perspective**.

You become the master of communicating your sentiments when you learn to be open and accurate without blame or judgment. In the constant art of **spoken truth**, you find emotional stability brings trust and compassion from others. Your integrity is at stake if you abandon, deny, and repress your feelings in favor of an illusion that passes for **expressive affection**.

You become whole when you reflect your inner feelings to the outside world. Your entire perception becomes discerning to the ways of spiritual deception. You are no longer fooled by those who would do you harm. In turn, you can offer **emotional healing** to those wounded souls.

The Queen of Cups' shadow could lose control of emotions and become overly sentimental, perhaps even maudlin, in your efforts to connect with others. A fine line exists between detachment and over-involvement, as either extreme is unacceptable.

Indifference breeds disconnection, which in turn brings coldness and unkindness toward others. Being too emotionally invested in the outcome can turn to manipulation and addiction. Seeking to balance the emotional heart with a grounded body takes practice.

The Queen of Cups' challenge is to examine her sacred wounding. These traumas bubble to the surface when least expected and create a tsunami of overwhelming emotional reactions. As she peers into her soul mirror, she sees the shadow that keeps her from healing. She understands arguing the point is unnecessary. She needs only to understand it to begin the process of recovery.

As she gazes into the pool of water, she feels herself detaching from the issues. There is no reason to relive the pain. She restores her divine gift of integrity and compassion for all living things by discovering the sacred medicine the wound offers.

The medicine was always there, but she was blind to it. She used her defenses to protect herself, thereby blocking her caring presence. She is the Psychic who feels too much. Once she surrendered to the understanding she did not have to hold everyone's pain, she became free to be the supportive Queen.

Step into the Divine and become the Queen of Cups:

The moon majestically edges above the horizon, cast in golden glory rather than the bright white of summer illumination. This full moon brings the season of the hunter into your awareness. You are called to higher consciousness—a risky state that opens you to emotional exposure.

This moon calls every wound you ever had into focus. You begin to understand that your identities are wrapped securely around old injuries, which keeps you bound to old expectations. What is real, and what is imagined? What is nominal, and what is high alert?

You must discover the Sacred Wound that drives your negative behavior. These deep-seated feelings are rarely what you believe them to be. To truly see them for what they are, you must explore the illusions you built to protect them. In doing so, you must also release the inner victim that accepted the responsibility behind the pain.

At this point in your development, you call upon divine stability—an open channel to your higher self— to give you the strength to rip away the layers and expose the truth. It takes enormous courage to peer beneath the surface. As you reach past the obvious and into the obscure, your natural defense system may block the pain that such severe wounding brings.

You rise to that higher challenge by acknowledging your maturity and all the difficulties in achieving such an elevated state of mind, body, and soul. If you can access your basic sense of personal integrity and embrace this achievement with pride, you can move onward and upward.

On an elemental level, this means allowing the waters of your emotions to flow freely without dams, levees, or any other kind of blocks to stop the powerful surge of unlimited healing waiting to happen.

The Queen of Cups offers the opportunity to recognize and act upon unconditional love through the expression of authenticity, thereby retaining the ability to love without reservation. A healed heart is open to many kinds of love.

Queen of Cups' Mantra:

"I see the great mysteries of life before me, and I am not afraid to explore the illusions that block my way to freedom. I am an emotional warrior ready to honor my authentic feelings."

The Heart Of Tarot

Questions from the Queen of Cups:

- What triggers a loss of emotional control?

- When have you been too invested in the outcome?

- How do you find the balance between detachment and investment?

- What brings unconditional love to the surface?

- What reflects your sense of security?

- How do you heal your inner victim?

- What is your Sacred Wound?

- How have you blocked your emotional development?

- How have you overcome your trauma?

- What is the symbol of your passionate warrior?

"Numbers, by themselves, represent universal principles through which all things must evolve and continue to grow in cyclic fashion. The Digits 1 - 9 symbolize the stages through which an idea must pass before it becomes reality. All manifestation is the result of these nine stages."

(*Numerology and the Divine Triangle*
by
Faith Javane and Dusty Bunker)

The Heart Of Tarot

Numbers Grid

Major	1	2	3	4	5	6	7	8	9
0	10	11	12	13	14	15	16	17	18
	19	20	21						
Minor	Ace/10	2	3	4	5	6	7	8	9

Numerology is an essential extension of Tarot. The above grid shows how the numbers line up in a deck and how the Major Arcana archetypical energies play with each other. **(Shadow is always the other 1 or 2 cards that support the main card.)** Note that there are only three groups that have three digits. Anyone who has a life/year number within the group has all three energies affecting them.

The other six have only two. The primary energy is the number calculated, and the supporting energy is the shadow card, often an unconscious or hidden aspect of that time. All the Minor Arcana numbers/elements reinforce the lessons and experiences of the Major Arcana.

By adding your birth Day + Month + Year, you discover the Tarot archetype that represents the energy you were born into and carry with you your whole life. By adding your birth Day, Month, and Current Year, you have the secondary energy that works in tandem with your life number for one year.

The year number can be tricky because it is subjective to the month you are born. The influence lasts from birthday to birthday and not on the calendar year (from January 1 to the following January 1.) For instance, if you add a birthday in September (9-16-2012), that influence will last until September 16, 2013. If you calculate a number for a person who has not yet reached their birth date, you will use the previous year.

For instance, let's say it is March 2012, and you calculate for someone whose birthday is February 14th. The date you would use would be 2-14-2012 (or the current year) and represent energy from 2-14-2012 through 2-14-2013.

However, if it is March and you are calculating a birthday for April 10 (which has not yet happened), you would use 4-10-2011. That energy would reflect from 4-10-2011 through 4-10-2012.

To look at the next numeric/archetypical energy cycle, you can go from 4-10-2012 through 4-10-2013. The archetypical number shows the existing or future patterns at any point in a person's life.

Dr. Ruth A. Souther

CALCULATING YOUR LIFE NUMBER

The Life Number is calculated using numerology. The corresponding Major Arcana card (Archetype) becomes the life-long guide and lesson on maturity. Add the number down to the highest Major Arcana, between 1 and 21. Look to this archetype for insight into success and failure, choices and opportunities, commitments, and indecisions. These tools review and point out changes to support growth.

BIRTH INFORMATION (Example: day+month+year of birth=sum)

DAY: 16
MONTH: 09
YEAR of BIRTH: 1952

SUM: 1977

Add SUM across: 1+9+7+7= 24

LIFE NUMBER: 2+4 = 6 (Lovers)
TAROT CARD: 6 – Lovers/Shadow – 15 (Devil)

SHADOW ENERGY IS CALCULATED UP OR DOWN THE MAJOR ARCANA BY FINDING THE EQUAL NUMBER. EXAMPLE: 1+5 (DEVIL) = 6 (LOVERS) OR 21 (UNIVERSE) SHADOW ENERGY IS 3 (PRIESTESS) 2+1 = 3

<u>BIRTH INFORMATION:</u>

DAY: _____

MONTH: _____

YEAR of BIRTH: _____

SUM: _____

ADD SUM ACROSS: _____

LIFE NUMBER: _____ (Major Arcana, 1 - 21)

TAROT CARD: _____ (Major Arcana, 1 -21)

The Heart Of Tarot

CALCULATING YOUR YEAR NUMBER

The Year Number is calculated using numerology; the corresponding Major Arcana card (Archetype) becomes the year-long guide. The Year Number is an additional way of taking stock of where you are going and where you are on your path. The influence is felt several months before a birthday and continues throughout the year. The Year Number does not take precedence over the Life Number; it works with those lessons.

BIRTH INFORMATION (Example: add day+month+current year=sum)

DAY:	16
MONTH:	09
CURRENT YEAR:	2012
SUM:	2037

Add SUM across: 2+0+3+7 = 12

YEAR NUMBER   12
TAROT CARD   12 - Hanged One (Shadow is Empress 1+2=3)

SHADOW ENERGY IS CALCULATED UP OR DOWN THE MAJOR ARCANA BY FINDING THE EQUAL NUMBER. EXAMPLE: 1+5 (DEVIL) = 6 (LOVERS) OR 21 (UNIVERSE) SHADOW ENERGY IS 3 (PRIESTESS) 2+1 = 3

BIRTH INFORMATION:

DAY: _____

MONTH: _____

CURRENT YEAR: _____

SUM: _____

ADD SUM ACROSS: _____

YEAR NUMBER: _____ (Major Arcana, 1 – 21)

TAROT CARD: _____ (Major Arcana, 1 – 21)

Dr. Ruth A. Souther

ASTROLOGICAL INFLUENCES

The Thoth-Crowley deck has astrological notations because of the author's interest in that particular metaphysical science. A few other decks indicate astrology within the symbols, but most do not. However, any deck can overlay this information to complement the original intention and as an additional tool for interpreting the cards. Below is a grid to quickly locate the astrological influence in any deck. The Royalty is not astrologically interpreted in the Thoth deck.

MAJOR ARCANA	PLANET/ SIGN	ASTROLOGICAL INTERPRETATION	#
Fool	Uranus	the development of individuality	0
Magician	Mercury	the development of independent tho|	1
Priestess	Moon	the development of emotional respor|	2
Empress	Venus	the development of emotional bonds	3
Emperor	Aries	the development of willpower	4
Hierophant	Taurus	the development of conscience	5
Lovers	Gemini	the development of communication	6
Chariot	Cancer	the development of survival tactics	7
Adjustment/Justice	Libra	the reconciliation of opposites	8
Hermit	Virgo	the search for purpose	9
Fortune	Jupiter	the expansion of confidence	10
Lust/Strength	Leo	the capacity for physical expression	11
Hanged One	Neptune	the insight of perception	12
Death/Rebirth	Scorpio	the intensity of awareness	13
Art/Temperance	Sagittarius	the gathering of information	14
Devil	Capricorn	the expression of integrity	15
Tower	Mars	the fortitude of courage	16
Star	Aquarius	the desire for freedom	17
Moon	Pisces	the association of instincts	18
Sun	Sun	the establishment of ego	19
Aeon/Judgment	Pluto	the recognition of integrity	20

The Heart Of Tarot

Minor Astrological Influences

ACE	No Notation	Fire
TWO	Mars in Aries	Fire
THREE	Sun in Aries	Fire
FOUR	Venus in Aries	Fire
FIVE	Saturn in Leo	Fire
SIX	Jupiter in Leo	Fire
SEVEN	Mars in Leo	Fire
EIGHT	Mercury in Sagittarius	Fire
NINE	Moon/Sun in Sagittarius	Fire
TEN	Saturn in Sagittarius	Fire
DISKS	**PLANET/SIGN**	**ELEMENT**
ACE	No Notation	Earth
TWO	Jupiter in Capricorn	Earth
THREE	Mars in Capricorn	Earth
FOUR	Sun in Capricorn	Earth
FIVE	Mercury in Taurus	Earth
SIX	Moon in Taurus	Earth
SEVEN	Saturn in Taurus	Earth
EIGHT	Sun in Virgo	Earth
NINE	Venus in Virgo	Earth
TEN	Mercury in Virgo	Earth
SWORDS	**PLANET/SIGN**	**ELEMENT**
ACE	No Notation	Air
TWO	Moon in Libra	Air
THREE	Saturn in Libra	Air
FOUR	Jupiter in Libra	Air
FIVE	Venus in Aquarius	Air
SIX	Mercury in Aquarius	Air
SEVEN	Moon in Aquarius	Air
EIGHT	Jupiter in Gemini	Air
NINE	Mars in Gemini	Air
TEN	Sun in Gemini	Air
CUPS	**PLANET/SIGN**	**ELEMENT**
ACE	No Notation	Water
TWO	Venus in Cancer	Water
THREE	Mercury in Cancer	Water
FOUR	Moon in Cancer	Water
FIVE	Mars in Scorpio	Water
SIX	Sun in Scorpio	Water
SEVEN	Venus in Scorpio	Water
EIGHT	Saturn in Pisces	Water
NINE	Jupiter in Pisces	Water
TEN	Mars in Pisces	Water

Dr. Ruth A. Souther

ASTROLOGICAL HOUSE SPREAD
(Represents where you are at this moment)

1st HOUSE – *IDENTITY* _____

2nd HOUSE – *VALUES* _____

3rd HOUSE - *VOICE* _____

4th HOUSE - *HOME* _____

5th HOUSE - *VISION* _____

6th HOUSE - *WORK* _____

7th HOUSE – *VENTURES* _____

8th HOUSE - *REBIRTH* _____

9th HOUSE – *BELIEFS* _____

10th HOUSE - *STATUS* _____

11th HOUSE – *DESIRES* _____

12th HOUSE - *SECRETS* _____

The Heart Of Tarot

Positional Meanings for Astrological House Spread

First House: Your identity, personality, or disposition

Second House: Your values, finances, or possessions

Third House: Your communications, written or verbal

Fourth House: Your home, family, or heritage

Fifth House: Your creativity, originality, or projects

Sixth House: Your work, profession, or vocation

Seventh House: Your partnerships, romantic or friendships

Eighth House: Your support from others, money, or investments

Ninth House: Your education, religion, or philosophy

Tenth House: Your reputation, social status, or business

Eleventh House: Your dreams, aspirations, or desires

Twelfth House: Your fears, secrets, or conscience

Dr. Ruth A. Souther

ASTROLOGICAL SIGNS SPREAD
(Represents your life at this moment)

ARIES - *I AM* _____

TAURUS - *I HAVE* _____

GEMINI - *I THINK* _____

CANCER - *I FEEL* _____

LEO - *I WILL* _____

VIRGO - *I ANALYZE* _____

LIBRA - *I BALANCE* _____

SCORPIO - *I DESIRE* _____

SAGITTARIUS - *I SEE* _____

CAPRICORN - *I USE* _____

AQUARIUS - *I KNOW* _____

PISCES - *I BELIEVE* _____

The Heart Of Tarot

Positional Meanings for Astrological Signs Spread

Position 1: Aries – your leadership role

Position 2: Taurus – your domestic task

Position 3: Gemini – your expressive position

Position 4: Cancer – your emotional nature

Position 5: Leo – your confident outlook

Position 6: Virgo – your industrious temperament

Position 7: Libra – your diplomatic character

Position 8: Scorpio – your determined strength

Position 9: Sagittarius – your philosophical spirit

Position 10: Capricorn – your resourceful ability

Position 11: Aquarius – your intellectual attention

Position 12: Pisces – your intuitive opinion

Dr. Ruth A. Souther

ELEMENTAL SPREAD

EARTH_____
What is my foundation?

AIR_____
How do I communicate?

FIRE_____
Where is my creativity?

WATER_____
When do I feel balanced?

SPIRIT_____
Who am I?

Earth represents physical life. It reflects the foundations you base your decisions on regarding home, family, health, work, and other concerns. This card can indicate issues with boundaries that keep you from starting or completing an important project. It can also point to the positive, healthier manner of establishing your identity. **What is your foundation?**

Air represents your voice. It reflects the mental processes by which you describe yourself and others. This card can indicate issues caused by non-constructive cognitive processes that keep you from speaking your truth. It can also point to a positive, more logical way of sorting through problems and offer constructive ways of airing your concerns. **How do you communicate?**

Fire represents authentic transformation. It reflects the process that gives birth to your creativity. This card can indicate where inspiration comes from and also where inspiration is blocked. It can also point to the positive, highly energetic drive that pushes change forward and allows you to fulfill your vision of the future. **Where is your creativity?**

Water represents emotional health. It reflects the process of assessing relationships and your bonds with others. This card can indicate the depth of your feelings and the area where you need to find emotional balance. It can also point to the positive way you find great joy, laughter, and those things that soothe your soul. **When do you feel balanced?**

Spirit represents intuitive insight. It reflects the process of intuitive knowledge and your ability to perceive the world around you. This card can indicate an unwillingness to see who and what surrounds you. It can also point to the optimistic, spontaneous, and discerning person you are evolving into. **Who are you?**

The Heart Of Tarot
INTUITIVE TAROT SPREAD

DATE: _____

CARD DRAWN: _____

WHAT IS THE FIRST THING YOU NOTICE? _____

WHAT IS THE PREDOMINATE COLOR? _____

WHICH ELEMENT FEELS THE MOST COMFORTABLE?_____

    AIR/MIND REPRESENTS THOUGHTS AND COMMUNICATION
    FIRE/SPIRIT REPRESENTS INTUITION AND CREATIVITY
    WATER/HEART REPRESENTS EMOTIONS AND HEALING
    EARTH/BODY REPRESENTS FOUNDATIONS AND BOUNDARIES

HOW DOES THIS ELEMENT SPEAK TO YOU? _____

WHAT SPECIFIC SYMBOL ARE YOU DRAWN TO? _____

WHAT IS THE IMPORTANCE OF THAT SYMBOL? _____

WHAT SYMBOL DO YOU FIND MOST DISTURBING? _____

HOW DOES THIS SYMBOL RELATE TO YOU? _____

WHAT SYMBOL IS MOST CALMING? _____

HOW DOES THIS SYMBOL RELATE TO YOU? _____

HOW DOES THIS CARD MAKE YOU FEEL? _____

_____

IF THIS IMAGE COULD TALK, WHAT WOULD IT SAY? _____

_____

CHOOSE ONE WORD TO DESCRIBE YOUR IMPRESSION OF CARD. _____

WHAT IMPACT DOES THIS WORD HAVE IN YOUR LIFE? _____

_____

_____

Dr. Ruth A. Souther

CELTIC CROSS/PATHWAY

1. HEART (Center card)   Emotional Truth
2. ISSUE (Card that crosses you)   Concerns/Problems/Questions
3. MENTAL (Card above you)   Communication/Thought
4. PHYSICAL (Card below you)   Foundations/Boundaries
5. PAST (Card to your left)   Lessons/Experience/Knowledge
6. FUTURE (Card to your right)   Possibilities/Choices/Prospects
7. CLARIFYING (1st card in path)   What do you need to know?
8. CLARIFYING (2nd on pathway)   What are your expectations?
9. CLARIFYING (3rd on pathway)   What supports you?
10. SUMMARY (4th on pathway)   The primary focus

Spread can be only the first six cards (the Celtic Cross)
Or can be accompanied by
the Pathway (cards 7-10) for additional information.

The Heart Of Tarot

THE YEAR IN MOTION: 24 CARD SPREAD

The Year may begin either on January 1, as a New Year projection, or as a spread to coincide with a birthday or other significant anniversary. Two cards are selected each month and can be done either as a blind draw (face down) or as a conscious draw (face up and chosen intentionally). Both ways are powerful and bring significant symbolism to the spread.

Many issues throughout the walk of life need to be sorted out. This spread sorts out the confusion. It is also used to chart your journey with ups and downs represented during the year.

The cards are placed in a big circle, going clockwise, with the first card drawn representing the **issue** of that month and the second card as the **solution**. These symbols are not conclusive; they do not define fortune-telling but rather the psychology of your unconscious mind.

You are likely aware of the issues and know what to do about the situation. Tarot merely highlights your instinctual knowledge, brings ideas to the forefront of your thoughts, and gives insight into your actions.

The spread just as often shows happier moments as the difficult ones. It also warns about the excesses humans tend to lean toward. The spread is not to be taken as an absolute fact but as an opportunity to work through the complications in your life.

Remember, Tarot represents the deeper Self and speaks to you as the oracle who provides choices and gives awareness. It is truly up to you to decide which way you go, how you feel, what is essential to speak aloud, and what your authentic self will reveal.

The Year in Motion

BONUS SECTION

The Fools' Journey
Written by Cynthea Jones

The Fool's Journey is a metaphoric voyage through the Major Arcana. My friend, teacher, and mentor, Cynthea Jones, wrote it in the early 1990s. It expresses the sentiments so well that I requested and received permission to reprint it here.

The story has been modified from the original script to work within a printed format. This extraordinary piece was created as a live meditation with parts spoken by many people.

The Fool's Journey
By Cynthea Jones

A presence steps into the center, a whimsical being, neither man nor woman, an image of innocence not embodied in sexual identity. You have a sense of fun and chance. You feel childlike in the presence of this person. Shy yet excited by a sense that anything could happen. This person turns to you and smiles, which warms you and removes all fear.

You know you are expected and welcomed by this being.

The Fool speaks:

"Welcome. Welcome to this place where Tarot lives. I am the Fool. I am spontaneity and foolishness. I am the impulse of your spirit. Yes, I am the one who takes you off cliffs, lets you fall in love, and puts you at risk, but I also connect you with your soul, with your aliveness.

How do you imagine me? How do you imagine the child who sees the truth, the naïve dreamer, the youngest one in the fairy stories who saves the kingdom and talks to the animals?

I want to give you the gift of innocence, hope, and foolish daring. Call on me, and you will invite pure spirit to dance in your dream.

I will tell you a secret: **I AM YOU**."

The Fool, the innocent one, steps up to you and dissolves into you. A voice inside you says, "Come with me. You will begin the Fool's Journey. The journey through life. The journey of the Self."

Into your vision steps a Magician, a person with the symbols of magic. How does the Magician appear to you? Let him take full form in your imagination. What tools does he have? How do you know he is magic?

The Magician speaks:

"I am the Magician. Magical thinking, magical speaking, magical action. The transformation of life comes through me. I direct energy into form with my magic wand. I am the original idea. I am action. I know the laws of the Universe and see the relationship of things unseen; therefore, I create Magic.

I communicate. I am the word, spoken and released. I know the power of the symbols and magical tools that the innocent Fool, pure spirit, brought into life. Magic words, I see the power of language. Words have the power to transform life when spoken aloud.

I am talented. I know what to do with the four elements: Fire, Water, Earth, and Air. I know what is essential. I hold a place in earthly life, and divine energy is channeled through me. I am your Self-Definition, your 'I AM' statement.

All I have described is part of you; after all, **I AM YOU.**"

The Magician walks to you and merges with you. You find yourself in a mist. As the mist begins to clear, you see a lovely woman standing before you. Mystical, mysterious, silent. The Moon and Stars are in her hair. Her silence seems to envelop you. She is a Priestess of an Ancient Order.

The Priestess speaks:
"Your awareness of me will connect you with the knowing deep within you, the knowing of your species. I am the Feminine, the Yin energy of receptivity. I am your subconscious mind and connection with the past. All things instinctively known to humanity are known through me.

I give you duality, your knowledge of good and evil, life and death, masculine-feminine, self-other. I will provide you with a glance beyond the veil that weaves all dualities as one. I will take you between the worlds to the place that is not of this world but creates the world. Call on me when you wish to remember what you have always known.

Call on me, for **I AM YOU.**"

The Priestess dissolves in the mist, and in her place appears a lush, sensual woman, an Earth Mother with flowers in her hair and bare feet that are very comfortable on the ground. You are aware that the creatures of the Earth, the plants and animals, know her, and she knows them. They are her children. You are also her child.

The Empress Speaks:
"I am the Great Mother. I am the Garden in the fullness of Summer. I am the patient Winter, pregnant with Spring. Call on me when you want to nurture yourself, your dreams and creations, or the children of your heart.

Call on me when you want to move in the Divine Grace of Natural Law. The laws of earthly life will allow you to grow and heal yourself and to fade and die in the natural order of all life. I am fertility, passion, joy in living, and the lush chaos of the Emotional Realm.

I am the principle of Mother Love. **I AM YOU.**"

The Empress holds out her right hand, and the Emperor appears at her side. He reminds you of power, authority, a ruler, and a leader. He represents society's laws, yet he is a kind father. He is your power to protect yourself and assert yourself. He is the aspect of you that sets your boundaries and your limits.

The Emperor Speaks:
"I am your assertive Self. I am willing to be powerful and defend your castle and boundaries. I am society's laws. Many are uncomfortable with me, but I realize I am far more than limitations and discipline. I am the reality you know as form. I give tangible existence to the four energies that preceded me.

I am your voice of Authority. I am your voice of Authorship. I remind you of your right to tell your own story and be the expert on the subject of yourself. I am your right and responsible for knowing and saying what you need.

I AM YOU."

Hand in hand, the Emperor and the Empress merge into you.

Out of the circle that surrounds you, a teacher appears. A Shaman, a Rabbi, a Priest, a Buddha. His shape and dress vary in accordance with the requirements of your spiritual tradition. He is a person of religious affiliation who carries a symbol of spiritual knowledge and practice.

The Hierophant speaks:
"Call me when you want to be in tune with Sacred Law. I am the memory of your ability to hear the messages in the wind and the river. I will remind you to listen to the voices of your ancestors and your inner guides.

In ancient times, I was called the Hierophant. I was a servant to my tribe and the Great Goddess Demeter. I learned the mysteries of Life and Death. I spoke to the Gods and Goddesses, the forces of Nature, and brought their knowledge to my people.

I am here to offer you the meaning that transcends logic. I am here to give you a glimpse of the great mystery of your life and relationships. I am your Teacher and Inner Counselor.

I AM WITHIN YOU."

The Hierophant steps into you, and you notice you are now holding a key.
A couple appears.
Remember when you were in love? Remember the emotions that awakened within you? Remember when Cupid and his troublesome arrows threw your peaceful life into chaos? Remember the choices that love demanded of you? They are here to remind you. They are the Lovers.

The Lovers speak:
"You are the Lovers. You are the energy that awakens within you as sexual love, personal love, and the decisions those issues will always create for you. You are your need to be with another and your need to remain true to yourself.

You are the duality, the polarity, the Either/Or. You are the Yin and the Yang, Male and Female, Receptive and Aggressive energies with you.

You are both sides. **YOU ARE YOU.**"

As the Lovers merge with you, you turn to see a knight in shining armor holding the grail, the victor home from his quest. He is in a chariot pulled by strong animals, dancing and prancing in their place, ready to go but standing still.

The Charioteer speaks:
"Knight in Shining Armor—you all know me. I am the Charioteer leading the victory parade, the Hero and the Savior. Let me tell you my story.

I have harnessed these powerful creatures to my chariot. Energy and force, they take me out into the world. My work is to employ their powers, direct their strengths, and unify their actions so that they will move as one. They are the animal force.

So often, these energies are repressed until they take you on the ride of your life. My challenge, as yours, is to control them to move forward. Their names are Desire, Passion, Fear, and Anger.

Without them, I am stuck. If one of them overpowers the others, I will be dangerously off course. My work requires me to know them well and convince them to work together. When I do, I am a great force of change and new direction in your life.

But before you can go anywhere, I need to ask what you are committed to. Where are you going in life? And is it time to say giddy-up? Will you allow the forces of life and desire to move you into public view?

When you look at me, all you see is my protection. I am hidden within the warrior's armor. I am the principle of vulnerability hidden behind the hero's public face. I am the paradox of public life and private vulnerability. I am Change and Control. I am Motion and Stillness. I am Vulnerability inside Impenetrable Armor.

I am a paradox, a contradiction, a moment of victory. For some people, the quest ends here at this moment of public recognition, but not you. You will go on to another level of exploration and interaction. I am the piece of you that has to go on to balance a deeper understanding of yourself and life. You see, my cup holds the dream.

I am the dream of what you can become. I AM YOU."

Chariot, Knight, and animals move swiftly forward with grace and unity to join forces with you.

Wasn't he talking about his vulnerability, his fears, and his control issues? Watch him lead the parade of cheering followers in your mind's eye. When are you the one who leads, looking confident while inwardly managing the forces of nature, Change, and Commitment?

The Heart Of Tarot

With this challenge, you complete the first seven cards of the Tarot. You have explored the Major Teachers in the lessons of Self-Knowing and Self-Development. Undivided within yourself, you are ready to investigate the psychology of Life and discover the force that lies in your true nature, the same energies that are present in the world around you.

You enter the Realm of Interactions and Challenges of Earthly Life. All the people you have known come to mind—your past flashes before you, full of kindness and pain, given and received. You turn and see a balance scale held by the Goddess of Justice, Themis. One cup is marked Alpha and holds your past—everything remembered and not remembered from your beginning to this moment. The other cup, Omega, contains your future. The Goddess offers you the scale.

The Goddess Justice speaks:

"Take it. Take your life, past and future, into your own hands. Justice must begin with this truth. You are the Goddesses, Gods, and the Fates and offer your wisdom and guidance, and you attempt to fill us with your future, but you hold the scales.

Just or unjust, you hold your own life in your hands. Just or unjust, you have the world's future in your hands. You make the past out of the future, one day at a time.

Just or unjust—**Adjustment**—you must find your balance.

Take the cup marked Alpha, your past, the beginning. Take the sword as well. It is the power of discernment. Use them both. Choose what you will give weight to in your past, what you will allow to be over, and as light as mist.

Choose what you will release. Decide what limits you and hurts you. Those things: release them. The mystery of balance is that which you hold heavy in your past and yet is also a weight in your future.

Take my scales into your own hands. You now hold your past and your future. The sword is Judgment, your ability to make choices and decisions. Use it. Respond to the contents of your life. Take action and watch the scale bob and balance. The game is about choice and consequences. Is this fair? What could be more fitting?

I am the recognition of your power. I am you."

Justice is joined by a wise old Hermit carrying a light and a staff as ancient and as shaped by life as himself. Justice fades into memory, but you are stronger now. The old man smiles and nods with your gain in mind.

The Hermit Speaks:

"I am here to help you hold the scales. I am here to help you look through your past and create your future. You don't have to take on the task of balance and adjustment alone. I am with you.

I will prepare you for the journey to your emotional depths. I will prepare you for your exploration of the mountain's wisdom. I will prepare you for the vision quest, but you must go alone to find your answers. I challenge you to learn the sound of your heart and be filled with your breath. Discover the truth within your body.

My hand glows with the radiance of healing energy as I offer you the lantern. Understand that light is your light, the only source of illumination you need. The path you seek belongs solely to you, and with my guidance, you will not veer away from your destiny.

I am the reflection of your wisdom. I AM YOU."

Imagine yourself taking the lantern from the old Hermit. The light inside flickers and breathes. The flame dances. It seems to know its own source and grows brighter. You look up, and the Hermit is gone, yet you feel wiser and able to face the future. He has opened to you the undiscovered territory of your path. He is the principle of the Inner Journey. The times you have turned away from the world of events and actions to seek the depths of your interior experience.

You feel a sparkle of energy, and a new presence forms; before you stands a Goddess holding the Wheel of Life.

The Goddess Fortuna speaks:
"Where the Hermit is the path of introspection, taken alone, I am life, ever-changing. I am the Goddess Fortuna. I spin the great Wheel of Earthly Change and Cycles. I spin the world and bring in the seasons and the years. I spin the globe, Spring becomes Summer, and Summer turns into Fall.

I am the personal seasons, the changing fortunes, the natural and inevitable cycles of nature. If you know my patterns, I will give you hope when you despair. I will keep you humble in your moment of victory. I will whisper in your ear, as I have to kings, queens, and kingdoms and broken hearts and souls.

I whisper, 'This too shall pass.'

I am birth, growth, decline, death, and new life. I am the Law of Renewal. Every cell in your body knows me and knows I live in you.

I am the change you desire most, the spin of the Wheel. I am you."

Fortuna morphs into a great and noble lion, and you hear a great roar. You see a beautiful woman who is tawny and lion-like herself. They are both lustrous and glowing.

The Lady speaks:
"I am your Lust for life. This mighty lion is my friend. The powerful animal nature, instinctual nature, serves me. I move as one with the force of life, the creative urge. I am willing to be fully alive, fully human, fully animal. To many people, I am as frightening as the lion I ride.

The recognition of change and the patterns of growth free me. Everything will change in your life whether or not you claim your power and follow your dream. You all struggle with the beast within. I choose to make my life force my friend rather than my pet.

I carry the cup, the grail, the heart's desire, the womb of all creation high over my head. It leads me. I serve this force of creation just like the lion serves me. You are a trinity. There are martyrs by the side of the road, the voices of limitation, the cries of fear, the whispers of powerlessness that tell me to hide, to cover myself, to be less than I am.

I step over them. I am your personal power. I want your Luster to be seen. Ride forth with me naked, ready to be seen.

I am instinctual nature, your guide to truth. I AM YOU."

As the Lady and the Lion ride away, you feel the Earth move under the lion's heavy and graceful steps. You turn and see a man, suspended and glowing, hanging upside down from a great tree—the Tree of Life.

The Hanged One speaks:

"I am the Hanged One. I am life in suspension, a pause, a time for you to view yourself from another perspective. I am your moment of enlightenment. I am the moment you realize you have nailed yourself to a self-created reality.

I am the awareness of your limiting beliefs. I let you know when you are stuck in a bind, on a grid, nailed to the wall. Invite me into your consciousness, and I will take you deep into yourself and your patterns. I will stand you on your head so that you will see another view of your life.

With this knowledge, you can free yourself or remain 'nailed.' The snake, change, and regeneration are at your head and feet. Free yourself from the grid. Shedding and growing await you. I am the moment that you understand your patterns.

I am perspective. I am the choice to embrace freedom. I am you."

The Hanged One points in the opposite direction, to his brother, the one who can best assist you in this change. A bare-bones skeleton with a Phoenix rising from his head appears.

Death speaks:

"I am Death, brother of the Hanged One, the enlightened one. Invited or uninvited, I come to you. I am Death. I am Transformation, brother of Enlightenment. I am the dance of liberation that follows knowing. I will take you back to the bare bones, to the skeleton structure that gives your life its form.

The Phoenix, Rebirth, rises from my head. I use your past to enrich the soil. I cut the strings that imprison your future. So you want transformation, but not quite in this way? You want freedom from your limitations, but you want another way to get there?

All I ask is for you to give up what is no longer needed and that is no longer useful. All I ask is that you die.

I am the release from your old patterns, the promise of Rebirth. I AM YOU."

Darkness engulfs you. This is the moment of death—the death of your old ways of being, of seeing yourself, of holding your world and the people who share it with you. This darkness is the end, the end of a cycle. Thirteen.

You are experiencing the power of the thirteenth moon. To the ancients, the cycle is complete. The depth of this moment is filled with eternity or infinity. Are you buried in the Earth, or are you the seed in the womb of the Mother?

Thirteen. This is not the final lesson; it is just the passage to another teaching. The light of a new day is beginning to break. Dawn, the sun is rising. In this new light, you see a radiant, angelic figure.

The Alchemist speaks:

"I am Art. I was freed at the moment of your release. I am the moment beyond death, beyond your fear of death, beyond all fear. I am your rebirth. I am just as you truly are.

I hold the cups of Fire and Water. I mix and blend the elements of your dreams, the power of your imagination, and the greater mythological story of you with the waters of time and the blood of your own body. Fire and Water. Imagination and Emotional Intensity. I am the ancient alchemist who mixes your visions and aspirations with the wellspring of existence.

These are the forces of the unseen, interior Self that creates life anew in the world of Earth and Air. Rebirth happens here, and I am its angel and its artist. I am your memory of all that you can be. I am your realization of the magic of the subconscious forces that create an authentic Self.

You have allowed limitation and belief in the world of form to die. I will accompany you on into the next spin of the spiral of becoming. You have met the forces of life and found lessons that you learn with others mirrored in the Inner Realms. Now you will go on to dance in the sky, to find your relationship with the Universe.

I am the emergence of your Authentic Self. I believe. I am you."

In the first seven cards, you discovered the individual. Then, you discover the individual in earthly life, journeying within and learning the lessons of the cycles of life. Now, you will explore your relationship with the Universe.

You find yourself on the path to higher consciousness, the path to unity described in the last seven cards. The trail appears before you, and a creature appears as you take the first few steps. It is a horrible-looking beast held on a leash by the mythical half-man, half-goat, Pan.

Pan is the God of Spring and Fertility; he plays the pipes for the nature nymphs to dance in the fertile growth of a new season. He stands silently before you and nods at his companion.

You look at the beast, the awful, frightening, pathetic, unexplained presence blocking your way. Why is this thing here? Why does it keep you from the angel's promise of deliverance? Why is this creature your first encounter on the passage to higher consciousness? Pan offers no more than a devilish grin as you continue to stare at the beast, twisted and awful.

The Beast speaks:
"I am you. I am your unclaimed self. I am the piece of you that you could not love, would not claim, would not admit to, and therefore, integrate and heal. I am your anger, unexpressed. I am your pain, unhealed. I am your first encounter with the experience of higher consciousness.

I am your humanness judged not worthy. You see me in others and the mythology of life around you. I am all things awful and segregated and therefore not included, not acknowledged, not healed. I can be seen for who I truly am, represented not by the things that bind me in darkness but by laughter and light.

I am free from judgment, free from exclusion. Free. I am you."

You look at the awful, misshapen Beast. You see his ugliness, and your heart breaks for his loneliness. You put out your hand to him, forgetting your fear in the presence of his pain. He comes to you, and when you touch him, his shape begins to change. Standing in your awareness and recognition, he becomes more beautiful and more beautiful until he is your angel's perfect image.

The beast spreads out his arms, and his arms become the magnificent wings of a butterfly. One leap, and he flies, soaring higher and higher. Pan laughs, the sound echoing in your ears as your gaze follows the butterfly's flight through the blue sky to a lovely tower. Perhaps an ivory tower. Perhaps not. What a great tower, you think. Someone really talented must have built it. You might even recognize it.

As you approach the building, you begin to feel fear and apprehension, but it is difficult to know why. You see the butterfly as it goes into the top window, and you notice there are no doors.

No way in.

Suddenly, you find yourself transported into the Tower.

No way out.

Now you understand your uneasiness. This is your tower. The structure you built around you to make yourself safe, secure, and unknowable. You look around and notice what pieces of your life you used to build it. Who is in your tower? Who is locked out? What in your life did you create that now imprisons you?

How will you feel after a month in this tower? How will you feel after a year? And another year? Will you forget there was an outside? How will you get out? Do you want out?

The Tower speaks:

"Each of these bricks was lovingly made by you, mortared into place by your own experiences. These were all choices made to shelter you from the pain of the outside world, from those who might see you as ugly and beast-like. They were made only to protect you.

It is beautiful here in this place you built, quiet, isolated from the challenges of expressing your authentic self. Here, you do not have to pretend or hide behind the façade of a beast. Whatever drove you into this Ivory Tower was all for your good, to stay sane and safe behind my walls. I am not a prison; I am reliable. You know my boundaries. It is here you ponder the greater meaning of life and the motivation of others. Stay with me, and I will always take care of you.

I am self-control and self-protection. I am safety. I am you."

The sky through your small window begins darkening, and the first shades of doubt color your thoughts. Take no action? Stay within these walls? You hear the sound of thunder. The sky gets darker and darker. A storm is coming. Lightning crashes all around you, and suddenly, your tower is destroyed. Your safety is ripped away. You are falling.

You are again free. You find yourself on Earth. Your security is gone, but you feel your feet on the ground. Look at your feet. You are standing in beautiful crystals. Look up. Beautiful stars in the night sky.

You are also a Star. You kneel and look into a pool of still water and see your radiant reflection. The reflection smiles back at you.

The Star speaks:

"You are the main character in your own story. You are the Star in your own life. You may value, love, and care for others, but you are the only one you truly have power over. The only one that you can make happy.

You are the Star in your own life. Your world revolves around you. You see from your perspective. It is time for you to claim this truth. It is time. Own your life, be yourself, and let your beauty be seen. I am your reflection.

I am the Sacred Dreamer within you. I am the piece of you with her head in the Stars and her feet on the Earth. My toes are in the waters of emotion and contact with the knowledge of your soul. I bring the dream to Earth, and Earthly life blooms from my gifts.

I am the impossible dream that becomes real. I am you."

The Heart Of Tarot

You look to the night sky and see the Star's beauty. You add your light to the great fabric of the Universe, knowing that you have a right and a responsibility to shine with all the other Stars.

The full Moon is rising. The landscape around you takes on a brightly lit night's mysterious, fluid shapes. You become aware that you are in the presence of the Moon Goddess.

The Moon Speaks:

"I am the Moon. I am Myth and Metaphor. I am the symbol in your dreams. I am your unconscious mind, your fears, your insanity, your spontaneous knowing, and your intuition. Men and dogs have howled at me for centuries, for eons, and I do not alter my course or my gifts.

I pull the tides, and the mighty oceans follow me. Think of my effect on you. I create madmen, geniuses, and mystics. I will speak to you in your dreams and visions. You and I, together, design your life and your experiences. Know me, and you will work in unison. Sit in the stillness and know the power of your personal myths and the metaphor of your being.

I am authenticity and obsession. I am the cycle of life. I am you."

The night passes, and the birds begin to sing. The sky is turning pink. Light begins to fill the world. Everything is crystal clear, and once again, you can plainly see. As the sun rises, you notice you are in a garden, a sanctuary, a safe place unrestricted by walls. You are a child free to play, dance, laugh, and experience joy and vitality.

The Sun speaks:

"I am the Sun. Grow. Open. Bloom. I call you into consciousness. I give you warmth, vitality, and energy. You are a child of the Universe, Innocent, without guilt, without fault. You are here in this earthly garden, living your personal story. As you grow into awareness, so does the world around you.

As you heal your conflicts and share your victories, the world's garden fills with new knowledge. You contribute through your journey. You are the stuff myths are made of, and the future is built upon the material of life.

I ask that you see yourself from my perspective. You are one of my children, like the flowers, like the animals, a creature of the Earth living the Laws of Nature, growing into full Self-Expression. Add your light and consciousness to the garden. Dance in the sunlight.

Look at this wonderful, rich world around you. Fully play in the Garden of Life. Do you really have anything better to do?

I am the Universal flow of energy that sustains life. I am you."

Another child now walks into your garden. You remember yourself. Aspects of yourself you were not utilizing have reawakened. You recall those lost moments. It has been a long journey to this garden. The child before you is full of potential. All your buried skills and sleeping knowledge are present before you, calling you to claim your totality.

The Aeon speaks:

"I am the child of your reawakening. You have experienced the journey through life, meeting and dancing with the different parts of yourself. You have sat in judgment of your choices, decisions, fears, and dreams and found yourself again and again in the form of others. I am the child of your integration.

I invite you into another way of being. I invite you to join me in the creation of a new Age of Consciousness. Join me. All is new and fresh to me. I am free from boxes and labels, isolation, and discouragement. Join me, let's play."

The child walks into a swirling tunnel of light, a portal to nowhere, to anywhere. You hear him call you, call your name.

"Come with me. Join me. Be one with me. Be all you are, and you will create a new world—a new reality.
I am the call to a higher purpose. I am integration. I am you."

Of course, you don't want to go, and of course you do. You step into the tunnel of light, pulled by the forces of nature and your own being. You are engulfed in movement, stars, pressure, and motion. You see that you are naked, exposed to the world without shame, and willing to be seen.

You are dancing on the head of a giant snake.

The Universe Speaks:

You are one with me. You have become the Universe. You are the Universe. Nothing will ever be foreign to you again because you are one with all. There is no other. There is only you interacting with you in many myriad and fascinating forms and personalities. You know that life is the dream, and beyond this dream, there is Unity.

I am Oneness. I am the circle with no beginning and no end. I am you."

Suddenly, you are back in the hall where you first entered. The Fool is at your side.

The Fool Speaks:

"Now that you have experienced all of these aspects of life, self, and others, you are again the Fool, free of judgment. Free of self-judgment. Having met and claimed all these pieces of yourself, you are the Wholly Fool, seeing yourself in others. As you live this truth, you may be called a Fool by the pieces of yourself known as others, who have not recalled their wholeness.

You may also forget you are 'the Fool' as you awaken from this dream. So, before you return, look down the hall and say goodbye. You look around the room, and all the Major Arcana, the Major Teachers of the Tarot, are present. They are all a part of you, within you, and available to you whenever you invite them into your life.

They say to you:

"Thank you. Thank you for being. Thank you for taking the Fool's Journey. Your life is the vehicle that provides us with your life, your means of existence and expression. You allow humankind to grow into awareness through the dance of your life. **You are the Dancer. You are the Dance.**"

You begin to dance. You move to the rhythms of the Universe, moving to the music of your own heart. You notice the similarity of your beat to all the other beats, and yet you are unique. As you leave this shared dream, you realize the wonder of who you are. The Major Teachers of the Tarot are full of life and ever present in the richness of your imagination.

Thank you, Cynthea Jones, for your dazzling, intense, and provocative conveyance of the Tarot. Without you and Patricia Storm, this book would not have been possible. Come to think of it, I would not be who I am today without all the experiences, love, and support from you and Diana's Grove.

Dr. Ruth A. Souther

Ruth Souther is a metaphysical and natural arts practitioner in Springfield, IL. She is a Master Shamanic Breathwork Facilitator, Master Reiki Practitioner, Hypnotherapist, Ritualist, Priestess, and Minister. She holds a Master's in Shamanic Intuitional Practices and a Doctorate of Shamanic Psychospiritual Studies and Initiated Priestess.

She facilitates Vega's Path Elemental Priestess, Universal Priestess, and Priestess Mystery School. She authored The Heart of Tarot (an intuitive guide to the cards), Vega's Path: The Elemental Priestess, and four novels: Death of Innocence, Surrender of Ego, Rise of Rebellion, and Obsession of Love, and six Anthologies to date: Shaman Heart: Turning Pain into Passion and Purpose, Shaman Heart: Sacred Rebel, Life-Changing Power of Self-Love, Mystic Memoirs: Beyond Belief Experiences, Chaos of Covid and Writing is Our Super Power.

She is a facilitating member of The Edge of Perception (NFP spiritual organization) and, along with other members, creates a safe space to offer rituals and ceremonies.

The Heart Of Tarot

In the summer months, you'll find her in Michigan at a family-owned cottage on Lake Gilead, surrounded by kids, grand and great-grandkids, and many cousins. It's her happy place where creativity flows just as the water ripples.

Reach Ruth at
ruthsouther52@gmail.com
www.vegaspath.com or www.Facebook/vegaspath
Edge of Perception | Springfield IL | Facebook
Ruth Souther | Facebook

Ruth is a contributing author and board member/Chief Editor of Crystal Heart Imprints—an independent cooperative press supporting and guiding authors and artists in their creative projects.

For more information, visit www.crystalheartimprints or Book Cooperative Association | Crystal Heart Imprints | United States.

www.ingramcontent.com/pod-product-compliance
Lightning Source LLC
Chambersburg PA
CBHW080634230426

43663CB00016B/2867